The Mystical

Exploring the Transcendent

Also available from the MSAC Philosophy Group

Spooky Physics

Darwin's DNA

The Magic of Consciousness

The Gnostic Mystery

When Scholars Study the Sacred

Mystics of India

The Unknowing Sage

String Theory

In Search of the Perfect Coke

Is the Universe an App?

Adventures in Science

You are Probability

The Mystical

Exploring the Transcendent

Mt. San Antonio College
Walnut, California

First Printing: 2014

ISBN: 978-1-56543-173-7

MSAC Philosophy Group
Mt. San Antonio College
1100 Walnut, California 91789 USA

Website: http://www.neuralsurfer.com

Imprint: *The Runnebohm Library Series*

Dedication

To our two boys:

Shaun-Michael and Kelly-Joseph

Table of Contents

Acknowledgements

Andrea and I would like to express our deepest thanks to Frank Visser and Integral World for publishing a large number of our articles over the years and for encouraging us in exploring the frontiers of neuroscience, quantum physics, and evolutionary biology.

The MSAC Philosophy Group

MSAC Philosophy Group was founded at Mt. San Antonio College in Walnut, California in 1990. It was designed to present a variety of materials--from original books to essays to websites to forums to blogs to social networks to films--on science, religion, and philosophy. In 2008 with the advent of print on demand and cloud computing, the MSAC Philosophy Group decided to embark on an ambitious program of publishing a large series of books and magazines. Today there are well over 100 distinct magazine titles and 50 book titles. In addition, the entire MSAC database is now being put online via Amazon's Kindle, Barnes and Noble's Nook, Google's eBooks, and Apple's iBooks. A special mobile app called Neural Surfer Films is now available for Apple's iPhones and iPads, as well as one for Android operating systems on smart phones and tablets. *The Runnebohm Library* contains works on Einstein, Turing, Russell, Crick and other luminous thinkers. Some of the more popular titles include, *Darwin's DNA: A Brief Introduction to Evolutionary Philosophy* and *Global Positioning Intelligence: The Future of Digital Information.* Finally, *The Runnebohm Library* is in the process of producing a number of highly interactive texts that will include embedded video, games, and interactive feedback loops.

1 | *The Mystical Dimension*

There is a Mystical Dimension that runs through all aspects of life. Eventually every human endeavor directly encounters an impenetrable Mystery where knowledge turns into ignorance and control into wonder. Indeed, no matter how much science or technology may advance, the essential mystery of life will never change. The reason why is simple: Reality is always greater than our conceptions of it. Thus, contrary to our popular notions of mysticism, genuine spiritual practice is not concerned with increasing knowledge, per se, but rather reconciling man with his fundamental state of absolute ignorance. We are born into a Mystery; we live in a Mystery; and we die in a Mystery. Although we may learn about things, achieving various levels of technical proficiency, we apparently can never know what a single thing is. For instance, what is a circle? What is a thought? What is a self? The essence of everything eludes us because our perceptions are always limited. As the late Baba Faqir Chand, the great sage of Hoshiarpur, once told me personally,

"Nature is unfathomable. No one has ever been able to know it completely. No one has known it. A small germ in a body cannot know the whole body. Similarly (a) human being is like a small germ in a vast Creation. How can he claim to have known the entire Creation. Those who say that they have known are wrong. No one can describe or even know the entire Creation. It is indescribable."

Often in the philosophy classes I have taught in undergraduate and graduate school, I would bring up this point of "unknowingness." Pointing to a crumpled piece of writing paper, I would ask the class, "What is this?" Almost in unison, the students would respond, "A piece of paper." Taking this as my cue to lead into a deeper philosophical investigation of materialism, I probed further, "Yes, but what is that?" Catching my drift, one student invariably answered, "Oh, it is actually a transformed sheet of wood."

Not wanting them to stop there, I asked, "And wood is made of what?" "It's comprised of molecules," the more scientifically oriented students would shout. Connecting to the now forgotten inner space ride at Disneyland, which takes one through an imaginary voyage inside a snowflake molecule, I queried, "But what is a molecule made of." By this time we had gotten down to the subatomic level, and our words began to betray our modicum of knowledge (electrons, protons, quarks, lucky charms, superstring).

The final question I asked was quite simple, but given the line of investigation it led to some severe complications: What is matter? Well, it should be obvious to the reader as it was to my class and to myself that there's only one truly appropriate response, "I don't know." Now, this is exactly the response not only of most mystics, but most quantum physicists as well. As Sir Arthur Eddington, the noted astronomer-physicist put it, "Something unknown is doing we don't know what!"

To be sure, mystics have said that the world (or matter) is nothing but consciousness. But, what is consciousness? Not even a sage as enlightened as Ramana Maharshi of South India could answer that question. To such queries, Ramana would often sit in silence. Ultimately, matter leads to consciousness and consciousness to God or Nature (with a capital N) and both to Mystery. However, no matter how you define it, slice it, categorize it, blend it, intuit it, the fact remains that Reality is a Mystery, and nobody apparently (not me, not you, not Einstein) knows what that Reality *is*. We are sitting right in the middle of the Mystical Dimension.

Yet instead of this Unknowable Realm being the basis for sorrow, it is in truth the foundation for man's freedom and liberation. Because by consciously surrendering to the transformative process of such native ignorance our lives become enlivened and informed by existence. A crude, yet perhaps accurate, example of this new kind mysticism (where science directs religion, and not vice versa) can be seen in the analogy of the ocean and the bubble. The ocean, in this metaphorical case, represents the total reality of all that exists (call it God or Nature or Whatever), whereas the bubble (our self or anything which is less than the totality of what arises) exemplifies a seemingly bound existence. Now as the bubble it has two primary options: 1) surrender to the ocean which is the creator, sustainer, and destroyer of its separate life; or 2) recoil and live in the (illusory) belief that as a bubble it has a distinct, autonomous existence. While both postures are not mutually exclusive, the unassailable fact remains that the former option is our necessary end game, whereas the latter position is to some measure our Darwinian necessity. It can be argued that "self" realization is when the bubble intuits its subservience to the ocean and that it has no real life except in relationship with the larger environment.

However, there is one very important catch here: the bubble (self) must be prepared to "burst" in the sea (Nature) from which it manifested. The ultimate physics that brought us into the universe are the same physics that will draw us out of it. The real dilemma, therefore, is not that we will die (that is inevitable, even if we can extend our specific lifetimes), but how we will choose to live in such existential context. In what ways will we confront the Mystery? In what ways will we seek to avoid it?

Recently, there has been a lot of discussion about how certain leading edges of science are re-discovering the Mystical Dimension. In physics, we find the strange world of photon entanglement; in neurophysiology, the processes of memory and altered states of awareness; in astronomy, the theory of black holes, antimatter, and inflating universes; and in biology, the intricate code of life--DNA--and the development of forms (morphology). But the rediscovery of that which remains unknown is a changing proposition and reflects more on our own limited cranial capacities than on what the universe or multiverse ultimately portends. In other words, the deep mystery we must first confront is epistemological. We have a tendency to conflate our neurology for ontology, and as such tend to inflate the world around us with our own unrecognized projections, which may or may not be accurate.

And since we are stuck to such map-making, we are circumscribed by a logical syllogism that on the surface seems intractable. All maps by definition are less than the territory to which they point (because if the map is exactly as large as the land itself, then such a map would be superfluous) and thus have "gaps." And if all maps invariably have gaps, then all such designs are inevitably, even if only partially, mistaken. What this means, of course, is that all the delineations we make about the world around us are potentially wrong because they are not perfect transparencies. This is why science always rediscovers the unknowable, because no matter how sophisticated our maps may be they will have a gap in them which will reveal something hitherto undiscovered. This is also why Karl Popper's notion of falsifiability serves us so well when appraising most scientific theories. We know a priori that human speculations (even if amazingly well grounded in physics or math) are always liable to error. It is this liability that, ironically, allows science to progress. A new technological product, for instance, isn't accepted as flawless but is rather closely examined by hackers and others to reveal some uninspected flaws. And because of this ongoing dialectic we have seen breathtaking changes in a variety of objects, from computers to cars.

All academic subjects have their epistemological cul du sacs. In math, we have Godel's incompleteness theorem which essentially says "consistency of such a system cannot be proved within the system." In physics we have Heisenberg's uncertainty principle (or relations) which simply states it is impossible to know with absolute precision the momentum and position of an electron, since the more certain you are about an electron's position, the less certain you are about its momentum (and vice versa). In astronomy we have the Einstein limit of light that tells us that we can only see so far with our telescopes within the parameters of relativity. And the list goes on. Science will undoubtedly expand our previous limits and horizons, but we will inevitably be stuck with our own neural constraints from the very beginning. And herein lays the great human dilemma: the limits of our skull are the limits of our understanding. Yes, we may augment our brains with artificial devices in the future, but even here we will only confront a new limit in time.

If we don't know what a single thing ultimately is (even if we can know various things about a material item, we are circumscribed in our knowledge about comprehending all of its various dimensions and interconnections), do we even know where we are ultimately? Yes, I may say something such as I live in Huntington Beach, but that is merely a section in Southern California which itself is part of a state of 50 in the United States which is part of a continent that is located on a planet that orbits a sun some 93 million miles away. However, where is that sun? It is but part of a galaxy which is part of a huge milky way which is expanding in a universe of untold size that some 13.8 billion years ago was collapsed into a space a billion times tinier than the 12 point size of the Garamond type on this page. Yet, where is that naked singularity located? Does it make any sense to even use such framing questions at this miniscule level? And, if some theoretical physicists are correct, then this universe of ours isn't singular at all, but part of a multiverse of unimaginable dimensions. Where are we has a simple answer it appears: *We don't know.*

What this means is that even if we forego religion and spirituality and opt for a purely materialistic understanding of what surrounds us, we are still touching moment to moment a mystery that transcends our ability to grasp it.

Which brings us to that most revealing of queries: Who or what is living us right now? Who or what is beating our hearts? Who or what is firing our neurons? Several immediate answers comes to mind, of course, ranging from Jesus to biochemistry, but when we closely inspect how our bodies operate we soon realize that our "I" has very little to do with the day to day functions of our life. We don't consciously grow the hair on our hands or digest our food. We witness something that supersedes us even as it literally lives us. Whatever that is, of course, is unknowable in its entirety. Thus, we don't know what a single thing is, we don't know where we are, and we don't even know whom or what is actually living us. We live in a Mystery, even as we act as if nothing is mysterious.

In fact, the Mystical Dimension (i.e., Ground of Being) is both absolutely immanent and transcendent. Itself being without form, though assuming form; without content, though manifesting content; without structure, though exhibiting structure. The Mystical Dimension is nothing less than paradoxical to the conventional mind, since by definition it both subsumes and transcends all conceptual frameworks. Ken Wilber describes it this way:

"The Absolute [The Mystical Dimension] is both the highest state of being and the ground of being; it is both the goal of evolution and the ground of evolution, the highest stage of development and the reality or suchness of all stages of development; the highest of all conditions and the Condition of all conditions; the highest rung in the ladder and the wood out of which the ladder is made. Anything less than that paradox generates either pantheistic reductionism, on the one hand, or wild and radical transcendentalism, on the other."

To face this Mystery is truly an awesome task. Imagine being set down in the middle of the ocean at twelve midnight with twenty to thirty foot waves and having no life raft. The infamous surf spot known as Mavericks, located north of Santa Cruz in California, comes to mind here. How would you feel? The very idea sparks utter fear in most of us; yet, right at this moment, as you read this page, the situation is not altogether different than that ocean. It is as if we are at an amusement park getting strapped into a new roller coaster ride and right before takeoff we are told by the operator that the ride ends in a ball of fire where we all die. Who could possibly enjoy such an attraction?

Yet, isn't this an apt description of our own present circumstance? We are going to end up dead no matter how much we squiggle and squirm and resist. Earthquakes, hurricanes, diseases, accidents, the list is exhaustless even if the final result is the exact same.

So, the real mystical question as we mentioned previously isn't that we are going to die (that is a certainty, even if we try to pretend otherwise), but how we are going to live in this temporary moment? That is the core of existentialism and, interestingly, the core of all scientific and religious endeavors. The beauty of the Mystical Dimension is that it cannot be prefigured. Or, as I often remarked in my Death and Dying classes, "If there really is a God (or Truth or Ultimate Concern) then He/She/It blows every conception that we have out the door." Yet, it is precisely this unknowability which constitutes our enlightenment. In every single moment of our existence we are seeing, feeling, smelling, hearing the Mystery. The ultimate truth is not simply an Other (although this aspect too cannot be denied), but He/She/It is also This: the chair, the bed, the sky, the toothbrush. And, in the midst of it all, we are natively ignorant. Such is the Mystical Dimension, such is human life. Indeed, the curious irony that awaits us is this:

The more we examine the mystical the more physical it seems; and the more we examine the physical the more mystical it appears.

"'Tis all Wonder, Wonder, Wonder; Wonder hath assumed a form"

NOTES

1. I owe my discussion here to the work of Da Kalki (alias Da Free John; Bubba Free John; Franklin Jones), particularly his books, *The Paradox of Instruction* (1977); *The Way That I Teach* (1978); and *Do You Know What Anything Is?* (1984); Nicholas of Cusa (See *Of Learned Ignorance*, translated by Father Germain Heron, 1954); and S.L Frank (See his masterpiece, *The Unknowable*, translated by Boris Jakim, 1983).

2 Quoted from the booklet, *The Master Speaks To The Foreigners*, edited by Professor Bhagat Ram Kamal (Hoshiarpur:

Faqir library Charitable Trust, 1978), page 7, which contains a partial transcript of my interview with Baba Faqir Chand.

3. Not surprisingly this lecture on "unknowingness," which I have presented to thousands of students has proved to be my most popular one. At the very core of our beings. there is both the intuition and the frank confession that we are but little children in the face of a truly awesome mystery (*mysterium tremendum*).

4 Quoted on the back cover of Ken Wilber's *Quantum Questions* (Boulder: Shambhala Publishers, 1984).

5 For more about this analogy see the chapter, "The Paradox of Da Free John," in my book, *Exposing Culls* (New York & London: Garland Publishing, 1993).

6. Ken Wilber, *Eye to Eye* (New York: Doubleday, 1983), page 293.

2 | *Speaking in Tongues*

The first time I heard of speaking in tongues was in 1972 in Brother August's sophomore religion class at Notre Dame High School. August had a deep interest in the Charismatic movement that had been sweeping through Roman Catholicism for the past four or five years. In class he played album recordings of Christians baptized in the spirit who spoke in glossolalia. To substantiate the phenomenon Biblically, Brother August often referred to *Chapter Two of Acts* where the apostles of Jesus became filled with the Holy Spirit and manifested a series of divine gifts. Although I found the topic of glossolalia fascinating, I did not really believe in it. Even at 15 years old I knew how easily the unconscious mind could trick us. Little did I realize that in just a few weeks' time I would undergo an extraordinary spiritual experience and speak in tongues.

It all began one night at Loyola University in southern California in March 1972. Brother August had been taking a large number of students to the weekly prayer meetings and masses held at the college. One day he invited my friend Joe Maria and I to go along. We agreed, not really sure what was in store for us. There were about 300 people that night. First there was some communal singing followed by testimonies by individuals who had been saved by Jesus and baptized in the spirit. The stories ranged from simple narratives of personal transformation ("I was trapped into taking drugs and the Lord helped me to see the light") to amazing accounts of physical healing ("I had cancer of the colon and the doctors didn't give me much chance for survival; I prayed to Jesus and felt infused with a wondrous light. When I went back for my checkup the doctors informed me there had been a remission. They just couldn't believe it. I could. It was the power of the Holy Spirit")

Joe and I sat there feeling a bit awed; obviously something tremendous was happening in these people's lives. After about an hour of singing and testimonials, everyone went to the chapel for mass. This was not the usual Catholic mass that I had been brought up with. There was no separation between the altar and the pews; instead both the priests and the laity stood together on the altar or right around it. It was a beautiful and moving celebration, unlike anything I had experienced before in my Catholic upbringing.

As the mass ended small prayer groups formed. It was at this time, I was told previously by Brother August, that the Holy Spirit really becomes active. I don't know why I walked up to one prayer group but I do know I was pulled by a higher impulse within myself. Personally, I was not interested in receiving tongues, a healing, or the gift of prophecy. I just simply wanted to know: What's really going on here? Is there a God? What's Truth? Who am I? The typical but nevertheless profound questions of most introspective teenagers.

The moment is forever instilled in my mind. I knelt down on the communal railings before four or five prayer partners and the leader of the Loyola prayer meetings asked me what I wanted. With all the intensity of my heart's quest, I said, "Just to know. I just want to know." I then closed my eyes and those around me prayed aloud. Then I felt the prayer leader put his hands on my head. Immediately I felt a surge of numinous power rush from the depths of my being. It was as if a torrent of radiant energy was rising from the core of my heart upwards. My entire body became flushed with a supernormal sense of warmth and peace. I felt incredibly alive and awake, as though everything before this moment was dull and dreamlike.

The prayer leader asked me to pray aloud but when I tried I could not speak. The mysterious presence within me took control of my vocal cords and my power of speech. Literally I heard some other force speaking from within the depths of my being. I was speaking in tongues. Nothing had prepared me for this moment. I never had imagined such a state of consciousness. All I could do in the midst of this spiritual glossolalia was laugh and cry, repeating mentally in my mind over and over again, "There really is a God. There really is a God." I cannot overemphasize the pure conviction and certainty which accompanied this baptism of the spirit. Doubt simply did not enter in. In that instant I knew what the saints meant by a mystical encounter; here was a reality far superior to the waking state, beyond the constraints of everyday existence. The phrases that issued forth from me were not consciously produced. Even to me they sounded completely foreign. Yet it was not just the glossolalia that affected me but the keen perception (bodily, mentally and spiritually) of a Being far greater than I. Rudolph Otto and Mircea Eliade have described the experience of Divine Energy as one of *Mysterium Tremendum* (tremendous mystery) and das *Ganz Andere* (wholly other). These two terms reflect both

10

the majesty and the distinctive otherworldliness of being baptized in the spirit.

The experience probably didn't last more than 10 minutes; I say probably because I had no sense of time during the mystical encounter. Finally, when I got up off my knees, several of my friends, including Joe Maria, came over and hugged me. They had seen what transpired and were just as amazed as I was. Brother August, who also witnessed the event, could not restrain himself; he broke into obviously joyful tears at seeing one of his own students receive glossolalia.

I couldn't sleep that night. My attempts to explain to my parents what had happened were fruitless. Who could blame them for not understanding their son's attempt to describe a transpersonal encounter with a spiritual being? Only my brother Joseph got a partial glimpse of what had occurred. As I walked into his bedroom, excited by the fact that I had spoken in tongues, I spontaneously went into glossolalia for a few seconds. My brother was astounded. Although he wasn't quite sure what tongues were, he knew that I wasn't faking it. The next day at school I became an instant religious "celebrity." Classmates with whom I had never spoken before now asked me for spiritual advice. "Tell me, Dave, what can I do to get tongues?" Tongues fever ran through the sophomore class. Glossolalia suddenly became wildly popular. In just a few weeks' time Notre Dame High School was having its own weekly prayer meetings on Friday nights. Because I had supposedly been "born again," Brother August asked me to lead the meetings. Attendance grew steadily, until finally the prayer gatherings reached a critical junction. Tongues fever reached its limit.

The meeting was packed with students, parents, priests and brothers. But the social pressure on the sophomore class to receive the gift of tongues was so strong that a number of students began to fake glossolalia to impress their peers and girlfriends. The whole thing turned into a fiasco. Dozens of students began pounding their desks in an emotional frenzy, praising God aloud. Yelping at the top of their lungs, these students were trying to imitate glossolalia. It was a farce and almost everybody there knew it. Soon afterwards the prayer meetings at Notre Dame were discontinued.

From that moment on most people at Notre Dame dismissed the whole phenomenon of tongues as a curious emotional aberration, a misguided attempt to display one's holiness. And to a large degree they probably were correct. For every genuine case of spiritual baptism and glossolalia, there were at least 10 that were not authentic. But what about the rare legitimate expression of glossolalia? What are we to make of it? Is there really a Holy Spirit ready to transform those who pray for salvation? Is speaking in tongues truly a sign of spiritual baptism? Authentic glossolalia has something more universal and structural to it than we may first suspect.

I have been asking these kinds of questions for almost 15 years. The answers are not simple. From my own experience, I know the phenomenon of tongues is more than just a psychological disorder or the manifestation of remembered preverbal babble. I am *not* convinced, however, that tongues is a unique gift of spiritual baptism bequeathed only to God-fearing Christians. Authentic glossolalia has something more universal and structural to it than we may first suspect. To understand what may be occurring let us examine closely what happened to me. First, I was receptive to my prayer partners. Regardless of what I ultimately desired, I was at least open to the possibility that my prayer might be answered. I remember being particularly sensitive that night. On the way to Loyola University one of my friends was being a bit obnoxious; yet instead of getting angry with him I felt I should be friendlier. It worked. Although this is a trivial episode, I nevertheless felt strangely uplifted by it, as if I had done something pleasing to God. This feeling of receptivity (no matter how fragile or deep), I believe, plays an important role in all mystical encounters.

Second, I did not yearn for any specific manifestation of God's grace, save that of knowledge. Hence, when I did speak in tongues it was a complete surprise to me. Naturally, this unexpectedness contributed to the feeling of *Ganz Andere* (wholly other). Realizing that I had nothing to do with the experience (i.e., I was not trying to imitate or fake glossolalia) also gave me a sense of mystery. Who or what was infusing me with such numinous energy? During the experience the answer was quite obvious: the Holy Spirit, God, Jesus. But these were all concepts that I had been brought up with in the Roman Catholic Church. Are tongues and the Holy Spirit necessarily connected? I think not. For example, glossolalia is neither original nor exclusive to Christianity. It is worldwide, in a number of different religions and cultures, many of which predate Catholicism. Third, I did not experience the spiritual baptism until after the prayer leader placed his hands on my head.

This would indicate (and would agree with the mystical schools of kundalini yoga and shabd yoga) that there was a transmission of some kind from the Charismatic leader to me, not unlike what occurs during initiation ceremonies in shamanism or guru-disciple relationships. It is important to note here that this particular prayer leader was well known for his gift of laying on of hands and as a catalyst for invoking glossolalia. And fourth, speaking in tongues was the after effect (not the cause) of a profound sensation of physical, emotional, mental, spiritual well being. Hence, tongues should not be thought of as the progenitor of my mystical encounter but the verbal confirmation of my inward state of consciousness. Most critics of the phenomenon confuse the two and tend to view tongues in isolation. This now leads us to the central question concerning glossolalia: Who or what causes tongues to occur? The Holy Spirit? The Higher Self? The Unconscious Mind?

Again, the answer is not simple. In some cases, especially when the person is emotionally unstable and susceptible, tongues could be the product of repression, a momentary outburst of the unconscious into the waking world. But this does not accurately account for super conscious experiences of glossolalia, where the person awakens to a state beyond the rational-verbal mind. In accepting an occurrence such as the one I underwent, we must acknowledge that there are higher levels of consciousness than the waking state. Indeed, as saints, mystics and yogis tell us, we have the inherent potential of experiencing extraordinary levels of awareness.

Is *speaking in tongues* merely a momentary outward expression of an inward, transpersonal state? In the case of genuine glossolalia I would argue yes. There is no evidence that tongues is a verifiable sign that God/Jesus/Holy Spirit has divinely baptized the person. Rather, only people born again within a Christian context use these terms. When a similar experience happens in kundalini yoga (a transference of shaktipat, for instance), the person inevitably refers to the language and concepts available within that system. In India they would call "tongues" a kriya—an outward sign of an awakening of kundalini (an internal evolutionary force within man). Thus, we can see that glossolalia (like the near-death experience) is a transcultural phenomenon, indicative of a higher state of consciousness available to all human beings, regardless of religion. But we must not go too far. True, tongues represents a level of awareness beyond that which we are normally used to.

13

Yet it is just a preliminary step in the higher worlds. It would be misleading to give glossolalia too high a mystical status, especially when even St. Paul did not give it preferential treatment. I think it is appropriate to point out that many people in the Christian world take tongues to be the be-all and end-all of spiritual experience; I found this to be the case especially in the Charismatic movement. Instead of viewing tongues as a very small advance into the mystical dimension, many take it as a final sign of their salvation. Such an absolutist posture ultimately leaves one stranded and unenlightened. I remember vividly, even at 15, arguing against this kind of perspective—to no avail. In fact, for this reason (the narrow purview of some born-again Catholics) I embarked on a comparative study of religion and mysticism.

No religion has a monopoly on truth, as the cliche rightly states. Therefore, we can see that mystical experience can be misused to serve outward, doctrinal purposes. For instance, when one undergoes the experience of tongues in a fundamentalist Christian setting, there is a tendency to attribute the encounter to Jesus/God/Holy Spirit (much as I did). Yet, as we have previously noted, this is a social categorization of the event and not one that is intrinsic to the experience itself. But because most individuals do not distinguish between structural (mystical) experience and cultural upbringing, they confuse and combine the two. It is perhaps for this reason that "born-again" Christians can be so adamant in claiming that the Bible is the only true Word of God. They have experienced a higher realm which gives them such conviction and certainty that they know it is more real than anything the world has to offer. Now, when this "transpersonal" encounter is connected to Christian dogma (due to the particular sociological setting), the person, knowingly or unknowingly, empowers his chosen religious belief. Hence, it is not necessarily the Bible itself that gives rise to the person's certainty of his faith but the direct, personal experience of a higher spiritual order. Furthermore, I would argue that most religious conflicts arise from the mistaken juxtaposition of doctrine and experience, where the former is given power and justification by the latter. Tongues is not the province of any one religion but rather the effect of a genuine mystical encounter which theoretically can happen to anybody, anywhere, anytime. But glossolalia cannot be literally translated like normal speech; in a sense, it is the mouth's way of expressing what cannot be truly spoken in words. I would argue,

14

finally, that tongues, as one of the "shells" of mystical experience, reveals outwardly what has inwardly transpired. As such, it should not become the object of exclusive glorification. There are innumerable levels of awareness to uncover in the inner journey of consciousness. It would be both a misfortune and a tragedy to mistake but a tiny drop for the entire ocean.

A FORTY-YEAR REFLECTION
How sex provided the clue to glossolalia

It has been nearly 40 years since I first spoke in tongues. It still stands out in my mind as a genuinely remarkable experience, though over the years I have developed a distinctive, if controversial, theory about what glossolalia ultimately indicates.

First, it is now fairly well known that speaking in tongues is not unique to the Christian Church. Second, the interpretation of what the phenomenon means varies within differing religious traditions. And, third glossolalia appears to be the after-effect of a prior internal state of awareness and not necessarily the cause of it.

However, when I was about 30 years old and living in Del Mar, California, another event occurred which transformed my understanding of glossolalia. It was rather late at night, perhaps around 11:45, and I was trying to get some sleep since I had to get up rather early and teach a morning class at UCSD. But all I could hear coming from another apartment was the moaning sounds of two people having sex. Now at first I was pleasantly bemused and thought to myself "oh this will last about five minutes and all will be calm." Yet, such was not the case, as the sounds (which oscillated from heavy breathing to dirty talk to what I thought were the sounds of a wounded hyena) didn't stop but got even louder and louder until finally after about an hour or so I yelled out the window, "Hey, put a muzzle on it, I have to sleep." This outburst of mine didn't help one bit, as the woman screamed back, "f.... sleep. I am going to c.... all night."

Okay, I thought to myself, this is not good. I tried putting a pillow over my head, but to no avail, as the pair continued at their nocturnal wrestling until far past 2 in the morning, which made me think that Superman (as she called her mate numerous times) was really alive and kicking in Del Mar.

In any case, right in the middle of these unedited proceedings I had a mini epiphany about speaking in tongues. Strange what late night thoughts you can get when you are sleep deprived.

Reflecting back on when I spoke in tongues the first time, I remembered that I was already in an ecstatic state before the charismatic leader and others asked me to speak out loud. What would have happened, I pondered, if I was never asked to say my prayer vocally? Would I have still spoken in tongues?

I don't think so. In fact, if I was in a different religious setting (maybe a meditation session), my focus would have been on the inner light that I was seeing or perhaps the intense heat circulating upwards in my body or perhaps I would have concentrated on the dissociative feeling that was arising.

Speaking in tongues was the outward manifestation of my internal state and, as such, was merely the vocal effect of an internal neurological state of being. This is similar, I thought, to what is happening in those engaged in sex in that upper apartment. Their ecstatic speech was merely the reflection of their sexual arousal and that the orgasm (no matter how loudly exclaimed) was the result of an internal body state, most acutely registered within the brain.

But in general nobody has sex so that they might get the gift of speaking in "orgasmolalia." No, what is desired is the sexual state itself and all that moaning and groaning and yelping is merely the outpouring of that prior state of bliss. However, in some Christian Churches, speaking in tongues is seen in isolation as if it were the end point or goal, forgetting that glossolalia is the vapor of an already achieved inner experience. I don't mean to suggest, in some neo-Freudian fashion, that speaking in tongues is the manifestation of some repressed sexual state.

No, I merely want to draw the parallels between two forms of ecstatic speech and ask the more pertinent question about why such language forms arise in the first place. My suggestion is that both arise because of internal neurological states, but that glossolalia is occasionally partitioned off and made into a sort of religious fetish that in some traditions can become ritualized over time. The outcome is that one might forget how glossolalia originates and what other possibilities the a priori state could have generated if the participant was allowed to focus his or her attention on some other feature within the mystical emergence.

One could, in fact, argue that speaking in tongues prevents one from actually going deeper into the altered state of consciousness, since it tends to force one to focus from the internal to the external precisely at the point in which the mystical encounter is starting to blossom.

I am sure there are gradations and exceptions to the above, but my hunch is that the reason speaking in tongues has been given such a cherished place within certain Pentecostal groups is because others not in such a state can witness, albeit partially, what would erstwhile remain private. Just as for some in sexual congress, the vocalization of their increasing sexual pleasure allows for the partner to better gauge and perhaps appreciate the intensity of the blissful union.

Transference and Projection: *empowering the written word*

Another aspect of speaking in tongues which I think has much in common with other numinous encounters is how easily it is to project and transfer such mystical happenings on to a holy scripture or personage.

For instance, the first book I was given to read after my born again experience was the Bible, but with specific instructions to read passages in the *New Testament* concerning the Pentecost and the gifts of the spirit.

This had the almost immediate effect of convincing me that the Bible must be partially true. Why? Because in the writings of Paul, in particular, I found a deeply resonant explanation of my own mystical encounter. If someone nearly two thousand years ago could understand what I was undergoing, then surely there must be some "truth" to it and explain why early Christian writings have survived for so long.

But this is a fundamental mistake that I soon realized just a few weeks after my glossolalia initiation. What would have happened if I were given a different book, one from a differing religious tradition that explained speaking in tongues in a variant way? Would I have then become convinced of the efficacy of that scripture as well? I think the answer is decidedly yes. Indeed, I have a suspicion that for many people who undergo a mystical encounter (and who are given holy texts within their culture to explain such apparent transmundane happenings) they, like myself, will have a natural tendency to empower the received text if such writing confirms and helps explain what had just transpired. But this projecting and transferring tendency (which humans seem almost predesigned to do) blinds us from other viable interpretations while at the

17

same time providing us with a palpable sense of certainty in the particular religious tradition.

Perhaps this can help us better understand why some Muslims, Christians, Sikhs, Jews, and Hindus can be so convinced that their respective holy books are true and are inspired by God. The mystical experience is so overwhelming and so extraordinary that when it is intertwined with a sacred scripture that contextualizes it, the would-be neophyte may then project and transfer his or her own certainty over to the text itself.

This conflation of one's own extraordinary experience with a revealed scripture can, in some instances, inflate the holy book itself to such heights so as to transform it too into an extraordinary and numinous artifact. We do this sort of transference all the time in our lives, but I think it gets deeply magnified when one undergoes a numinous encounter, even if such an encounter can be explained away by others as merely brain chemistry.

Another correlation between speaking in tongues and sexual talk that became apparent to me that night in Del Mar was that others who were not in such states of revelry could hear both. Because of this, one could easily mimic either state and give the impression that one was indeed undergoing a blissful encounter.

I first noticed this after I became the leader of the prayer meetings at Notre Dame High School. It seemed obvious to me, and was later confirmed by interviews after, that many students who claimed to be genuinely speaking in tongues were not. They were simply mimicking the process, primarily so that they could get the peer recognition of being "born again." It is relatively easy to echo glossolalia or even an orgasm (see the movie *When Harry Met Sally* for an example of this), and this may better explain the memetic propagation of each. My hunch is that one of the reasons speaking in tongues can at varying times become so sweeping and popular within certain Churches is not because each person is indeed having a mystical encounter, but because it can be so easily mimicked. In my own experiences at Notre Dame, I think I only met one or two other individuals (out of the fifty or so who claimed to have undergone the transformation) who I felt had genuinely spoken in tongues. And by genuine I only mean that they were not faking the process or trying to elicit the experience by intensive mimicry.

In conclusion, I think it is important to note that even if glossolalia is explained as a recursive throwback to our evolutionary past when language first emerged, or as an adaptive signal to confirm to others in our tribe that ecstasy is possible, it is a truly amazing experience and may be indicative of other more luminous states of consciousness within the human neuroanatomy.

The Following is an excerpt from **The Encyclopedia of Occultism and Parapsychology** (Fifth Edition)

The Bhrigu Samhita is an ancient Hindu astrological treatise, said to contain details of millions of lives, with horoscopes drawn for the time of consultation. The original Bhrigu was a Vedic sage and is mentioned in the Mahabharata. As the Bhrigus were a sacred race, it is difficult to identify the compiler of the Bhrigu-Samhita, but according to legend he lived 10,000 years ago and had a divine vision of everyone who was to be born in every country of the world. He compiled this information in his great treatise on astrology, originally written on palm leaves. No complete manuscript is known, but large sections are rumored to exist somewhere in India.

A printed version is said to comprise some 200 volumes, but most Indian astrologers who use the system work with loose manuscript pages. These are supposed to give the name of the client compiled from Sanskrit syllables approximating names in any language, with details of past, present, and future life, as well as previous incarnations. In addition to his fee, the astrologer usually proposes the sponsorship of a special religious rite to propitiate the gods for past sins. Indian astrologers reported using the Bhrigu-Samhita include Pandit Devakinandan Shastri of Swarsati Phatak, in the old city of Benares; and Pandit Biswanath Bannerjee of Sadananda Road (near the Ujjala movie house) in Calcutta.

In *Fate magazine* (June 1982), David Christopher Lane, a noted scholar of spiritual movements and cults, described a personal consultation with Hindu astrologers in Hoshiarpur, Punjab, India, who were custodians of a set of Bhrigu-Samhita leaves. At the time Lane was researching the Radhasoami movement in India, on which he has become a world famous authority. On July 22, 1978, Lane was taken by his friend Swami Yogeshwar Ananda Saraswati to a house in a back street of Hoshiarpur, where two astrologers had charge of a large set of Bhrigu-Samhita leaves tied in bundles. The astrologers first compiled a graph, rather like a Western horoscope, but featuring the date of Lane's arrival at the house. According to Hindu tradition, all consultations with the Bhrigu-Samhita are preordained, and the moment of arrival is the key to discovery of the correct leaf, which indicates not only the life pattern and destiny of the inquirer, but also his name in a Sanskrit equivalent of the language of the inquirer.

Lane stated that after inspection of various bundles of leaves, taken down from the shelf and examined, the correct leaf was found in about 15 or 20 minutes. Lane was shown the leaf, and the Sanskrit inscriptions were translated: A young man has come from a far-off land across the sea. His name is David Lane and he has come with a pandit [scholar] and a swami.

Lane questioned how his name could be known, and the swami showed him the Sanskrit equivalent of the Bhrigu leaf. The reading continued:

The young man is here to study dharma [religious duty] and meet with holy men and saints.

Other personal details were also given, including a sketch of Lane's past and present lives. He expected to be able to make a copy of the leaf with its reading, but to his surprise he was told that he could keep the original leaf. The astrologer explained:

"The Bhrigu-Samhita replenishes itself, sometimes with very old leaves and with some less aged. We do nothing; there is no need to. The astral records manifest physically at the appropriate time and place."

It was something of an anticlimax when the last lines of the horoscope stated that in order to expiate a sin in a previous life, Lane was advised to pay 150 rupees (approximately $20). But no pressure whatever was put on Lane to pay this modest sum, and the attitude of the astrologers and Swami Yogeshwar that there had been a divine revelation convinced Lane that this was no vulgar fraud. For such a small sum, the preparation of a fake Bhrigu leaf, and the willingness to allow Lane to take it away with him (and thus verify its antiquity) would have been out of all proportion to the work involved.

Moreover, the specific details of the horoscope could not have been known in advance of Lane's visit. Lane's experience was not unique, since a Canadian named H. G. McKenzie recorded that he used the Bhrigu-Samhita in the early 1970s and also verified its accuracy. He wrote: "I consulted Bhrigu-Samhita and found my name mentioned there, besides so many other things about my life that shows that one has no free will.... The Bhrigu-Samhita states about me that I, Mr. McKenzie from Canada, am here with such and such people. It states some events of my past life and also predicts the future course of my life."

In 1980 Lane met and talked with Anders Johanssen, a professional astrologer from Sweden who was then visiting Los Angeles. Johanssen stated that he had used the Bhrigu-Samhita at least seven times and was convinced that it was an authentic work and the most accurate treatise he had encountered. He believed that the copy in Hoshiarpur was the most complete, although other versions were known in Delhi, Meerut, and Benares. However, it was not clear what the nature of a Bhrigu consultation was on subsequent visits. If the leaf from the first consultation was freely offered (as in the case of David Lane), were other leaves available for each of the later visits? In Lane's case, his Bhrigu horoscope contained the prediction: This young man will come again several times.

On the first visit, Lane accepted the offered leaf, but left it with Swami Yogeshwar to make an exact English translation, planning to collect the original leaf and translation a few weeks later. However, Lane curtailed his trip due to illness and was later unable to contact the swami. Lane made a second visit to Bhrigu-Samhita at Hoshiarpur three years later, in 1981, in company with Prof. Bhagat Ram Kamal. He gave two days' notice of the intended visit, but no leaf for the visit could be discovered, arguing for the genuineness of the astrologers, since no fee was requested."

A PERSONAL ADVENTURE

In the summer of 1978 I went to North India with Professor Mark Juergensmeyer of the University of California at Berkeley to study the Radhasoami movement. The Radhasoami movement, founded by Shiv Dayal Singh (1818-1878) in the mid-19th Century in Agra, India, is a religious tradition based upon Sant mat, the "path of the saints." It has many branches, the largest of which is in Beas, Punjab, India. The basic tenets of the movement are: the practice of surat shabd yoga; the belief in a living Master who initiates disciples into the path; a pure moral life which includes the abstinence from meat, fish, eggs, alcohol, drugs and sex outside marriage; an the firm conviction that Jivan Mukti--liberation or enlightenment while living--is possible under the guidance of a realized saint or mystic.

23

It is of interest and usually not known in America that the Radhasoami movement has been the basis for several popular religious groups in America including the Divine Light Mission—Guru Maharaji's father was allegedly initiated by Sawan Singh of Radhasoami Beas and later left to start his own sect; Paul Twitchell who was initiated by Kirpal Singh, himself a disciple of Sawan Singh; and MSIA, founded by John-Roger Hinkins who claims to have been given permission to initiate devotees to the inner spiritual planes by Sawan Singh.

I was invited to go on the trip because of my knowledge of obscure yogis and saints in the region. My job was to visit the various gurus and ashrams in the Punjab and compile an exhaustive genealogical tree of the spiritual leaders involved in the tradition.

Later, during my travels alone, I visited with Baba Faqir Chand, a 92-year-old sage who had been doing intensive spiritual practices for over 75 years. He was regarded as one of the three most advanced adepts of surat shabd yoga in the world. It was during my stay with this venerable saint that I learned of the Bhrigu Samhita which is considered to be a physical counterpart to the controversial "Akashic Records"--a complete account of mankind's experiences allegedly existing in the astral and causal planes -- and the oldest astrological treatise in the world. On the last day of my stay at Manavta Mandir I was invited by my friend Swami Yogeshwar Ananda Saraswati and a local scholar to consult the ancient work. Although my time was limited I agreed to go.

On July 22, 1978, in the midst of India's torrential monsoons and intense summer heat, the Swami and I took a bicycle rickshaw from the "Be-Man Temple" and followed our scholar guide through the crowded city streets of Hoshiarpur to our destination. On the way Swami Yogeshwar told me the fascinating legend of the book.

Millenniums ago, during an untraceable time in India's history, the renowned sage Bhrigu reigned as the world's greatest astrologer. His mastery of astrology was so profound that he was able to dictate certain parts of the Akashic Records from the astral worlds onto special scrolls in the sacred language of Sanskrit, often called by Indian mystics "the language of the gods."

This primordial translation was said to contain the record of every human being who ever lived on earth. During each age the work has been transferred onto new leaves in order to preserve it for future generations. The present manuscript is said to be an exact copy of the original and is itself 400 to 500 years old. According to Hindu mythology Bhrigu was a son of the sage Varun. It is said that once Bhrigu visited Lord Vishnu when the latter was sleeping with his consort Lakshami. As Bhrigu was not accorded a proper welcome by Vishnu, the former felt annoyed and he hit Lord Vishnu. The act of Bhrigu was Intolerable to the wife of Lord Vishnu. She became angry with Bhrigu and cursed him, "You and your entire Brahman generation shall ever live a life of pauperism and Lakshami shall remain far away from Brahmans." Bhrigu repented for his deed and pleaded for mercy to Goddess Lakshami. Ultimately, the goddess took mercy upon Bhrigu and told him to write the Bhrigu Samhita (an astrological book) to earn his own livelihood and a livelihood for his generation, since it was not possible for her to withdraw the curse.

Where and when this book was written by Bhrigu has not yet been ascertained by any scholar. Because Braha and Utpal, the great astrologers of ancient India, make no reference to this book in their writings it is believed that it must have been written in the post-Vedic period.

The original Bhrigu Samhita has not yet been traced. It appears some parts of it are owned by Brahman families in Benares, Poona and Meerut but they do not allow anyone to study these chapters. Thus this great astrological book still remains beyond the reach of scholars.

Reference to Bhrigu Samhita is made in *Jatak-Skand*, which implies that the horoscope and the forecast of the entire life of every human being born on this planet is given in this book, according to the time, place and date of birth of the individual. Eleven chapters deal with different aspects of human life. These chapters are: *Kundli Khan:* horoscope *Phabit Kahand:* forecasts; *JarahParharan:* previous lives; *Tathalin BhriguPrashan:* questions of Bhrigu; *Nasht-Janmong Deepih:* index to lost horoscopes; *Sarivarisht-Nivaran-Khand*--remedy to human problems; Raj-Khand: pertaining to rule; *Santan-upaya-Khand:*for begetting children; *Narpati-Jayacharya Khand:* for the victory and works of a king Istri-PhabitKhand: on the nature of women.

I was told by Yogeshwar and by others also that this work in Hoshiarpur is the only one of its kind now in existence in India. Vague references to the Bhrigu Samhita appear in few books.

Dr. Paul Brunton, one of the first Western seekers to meet Ramana Maharishi and Anand Sarup of Dayal Bagh, knew of its existence in the early 1930's. In his book *A Search in Secret India* Brunton repeats a revealing conversation he had with the accomplished astrologer Sudhei Babu about the works of Bhrigu: "Do you know if there is any English translation of the Book?" Brunton asked the astrologer. The astrologer shook his head "I have never heard of one. Few even are the Hindus who know of the existence of the book. Hitherto it has been kept secret." "When was it written?" "It was composed thousands of years ago by the sage Bhrigu, who lived so long ago that I cannot give you a date."

Not being much interested in astrology and doubtful of its exactitude as a science, I admit that I took the legend with good doses of skepticism. The only propelling force in its favor was my confidence and trust in the swami and the scholar. Yogeshwar was a Christian monk extremely knowledgeable in Western science; the scholar was an expert in the philosophical systems of India. Their unremitting belief in the book's validity, which they claim resulted from their own experiences with its awesome accuracy, deeply impressed me. I attempted to keep an open mind.

When we finally arrived at the library that was sandwiched between two back streets, I was immediately struck by the large array of Sanskrit leaves tied in huge bundles. I had imagined that there would be one large book. Two librarians, who also were expert astrologers, were on duty. Apparently this valuable treasure had been a family possession for years. I found them intelligent, matter-of-fact and fluent in English. We enjoyed some chai (Indian tea which tastes like a cross between coffee and hot chocolate) as we discussed some of the implications of the work. The astrologers believe that nobody can consult the Bhrigu Samhita unless it is preordained. Therefore my coming had been expected and arranged for thousands of years ago.

Stories abound concerning individuals who have tried to reach the library but failed. Among the innumerable papers one particular leaf would be found which contains the details of my life, the librarians told me. A picture-graph was made by the astrologers using the date of my arrival at the Bhrigu Samhita as well as my birth date and birthplace. I got the impression that the most vital event was my arrival at the library. This event set all other facts into motion. The chart looked like a reconstruction of certain star, lunar and solar positions. My companions had complete confidence in the librarians' abilities. Using the picture-graph based upon my life, the astrologers were able to riffle through the huge stacks looking for a leaf that had the same chart drawing. This precise matchup, supposedly written by the sage Bhrigu thousands of years ago, gives in Sanskrit a description of me or any other person who has arrived and whose picture-graph has been computed.

I was told that it could take from a few minutes to a few hours to a whole day to find the appropriate matching horoscope. Curious about this unusual system I asked Swami Yogeshwar if the library had any classification system. He told me it does not and added, a little mysteriously, "They don't need it; it is destiny itself which guides them to find it!" Everyone got involved. Several bundles were taken down from the shelf at random and untied. The two astrologers, the swami and the scholar got busy looking for the corresponding chart. I began to feel it was a fruitless task. However, after 15 or 20 minutes the scholar exclaimed that he had found it. This, I was told later, was unusually quick; it added to everyone's sense of anticipation. The two librarians and Swami Yogeshwar examined it closely and all agreed it was an exact replica. This parched Sanskrit scroll would have the information on my life.

Examining the leaf carefully I could not help feeling an odd sense of providence. While the astrologers read through it Swami Yogeshwar and the scholar translated its message into English. When the first sentence was read I was taken aback. I noticed that Swami Yogeshwar and the scholar also were deeply moved. It was obvious, at least to those of us present, that this was real. The first line said,

A young man has come from a far-off land across the sea. His name is David Lane and he has come with a pandit and a swami.

I stopped the reading in mid-sentence and asked for an explanation as to how my name could be mentioned. Swami Yogeshwar showed me the leaf on which my name was written in Sanskrit and pointed out that the pronunciation was almost exactly the same. The scholar, although familiar with the Bhrigu Samhita, was also most impressed by its exactitude. But the astrologers accepted it as a common occurrence and read on,

The young man is here to study dharma (religion) and meet with holy men and saints.

Certain things of a personal nature were related which I found very touching; details of my present life were given and there followed a description of my past. Swami Yogeshwar wrote down the Sanskrit and partially translated it for me on a scrap of paper. But to my surprise, I was told I could keep the original leaf if I wished. It was then I heard this amazing statement about the book from the astrologers' lips, "The Bhrigu Samhita replenishes itself, and with sometimes with very old leaves and with some less aged. We do nothing; there is no need to. The astral records manifest physically at the appropriate time and place."

My doubt doubled when one of the last lines of the horoscope was read aloud. In order to rectify a sin I had committed in a previous life I was advised to pay 150 rupees approximately 20 American dollars) to the Bhrigu Samhita. I smiled, thinking the hour spent had been an interesting diversion--even if it wasn't genuine. But, interestingly enough, no pressure was put on me to pay the amount mentioned in the leaf. Rather, Swami Yogeshwar and the others said there was no hurry. I had no intention of paying the amount but I did find the librarians' attitude the opposite of what one would expect from those engaged in a con game. This, plus the euphoric effect the reading seemed to have on everyone present, prompted me not to dismiss it simply as a fraud. The swami acted as if there had been a revelation. Indeed, his own words to me were, "God has spoken today to us, dear friend, through the agency of the Bhrigu Samhita!" Also I have learned that the legend surrounding the book states that Bhrigu wrote the Bhrigu Samhita "for earning his own livelihood and for the livelihood of his generation." This would partially explain why the work has a built-in request for money.

For two years I have pondered the various explanations for the information found in the Bhrigu Samhita. The possibilities range from outright fraud to elaborate metaphysical theories. The more I doubted it the more my contacts with individuals and books seemed to attest to its authenticity.

A Canadian named H.G. McKenzie, for example, visited the astrological work in the early 1970's and was convinced of its accuracy. McKenzie wrote,

"I consulted Bhrigu Samhita and found my name mentioned there, besides so many other things about my life that shows that one has no free will...The Bhrigu Samhita states about me that I, Mr. McKenzie from Canada, am here with such and such people. It states some events of my past life and also predicts the future course of my life."

Baba Faqir Chand, a sage known throughout the Punjab for his extreme honesty and utmost frankness, also attests to the validity of the book. Faqir states,

"Everybody reaps the fruit of his or her deed. Major Som Nath of Aligarh is one of my associates. He came to me before the Indo-Pak war of 1971-72 and also went ot Bhrigu Samhita to consult his horoscope. They told him that he was a judge in his previous life and that he had accepted a huge bribe from a culprit and subsequently acquitted him and punished an innocent man in his place. As a result of this he would face a great danger to his life in that year. The astrologer suggested to him some Hawan, some atonement. But he did not perform it. However, when he went to his place of posting in the field he was directed to move to the forward post of Shakargarh with two companions. They traveled by jeep. Suddenly a mine burst under the jeep and they all suffered serious injuries. . . Now, had the Bhrigu Samhita astrologer not told him in advance about his forthcoming trouble I would not have commented. He did face a great danger to his life. This shows that our previous deeds dominate our present lives."

In 1980 in Los Angeles I met and talked with Anders Johannsen, a professional astrologer from Sweden. He informed me that after visiting Bhrigu Samhita seven times he is convinced that the work is authentic and the most accurate treatise he has ever come upon. Although I was told the book existed only in Hoshiarpur, Johannsen said that is only the most famous and complete copy--that parts of it also exist in Delhi, Meerut and Benares.

One can imaginE a scenario of possibilities to explain the Bhrigu Samhita's existence. The request for money to pay off a previous sin, which appears built into the work, may be a device to provide a livelihood for the librarians or the astrologers who wrote the massive book or who work with it. But this is common in many Indic traditions and does not necessarily invalidate the accuracy of the horoscope. The confidence and respect exhibited by all those connected with the Bhrigu Samhita in Hoshiarpur prompts me to look for a deeper explanation.

Scientists of both the East and the West have criticized astrology severely in the last century on the grounds that it is erroneously conceived and pseudo-psychological. And this well may be correct. As Dr. Lyall Watson perceptively observes,

"Even the most ardent devotees of astrology admit that their study lacks a clear philosophic basis, that the laws and principles governing it are still uncoordinated and that the records are scattered and contain many errors."

29

But the most important point in astrology is often overlooked or sidestepped. All disciplines--philosophic or scientific, from subatomic physics to music theory--have something in common with astrology. They are all communication vectors, information channels. Astrology, although not usually thought of as such, is a highly refined language code almost universal among advanced civilizations. Because of this astrology has survived. Mathematics, chemistry and social sciences are also language models (communication operators) and in this regard are much like astrology. The underlying fundamental in language (and in all science and philosophy) is the notion of intention. Without intention all systems are without meaning.

Astrology may never be vindicated by the disciplines of physics or astronomy, precisely because it is not so much a scientific discipline as a religious system, where intention and myth making hold sway. I say this because astrology today (especially as practiced by most people in India and America) does not subject itself to wholesale criticism; rather, it tends to act dogmatically in relying on so called "revealed" explanations of star and planet positions and their respective interpretations. As such, astrology is not a science, but a religious/psychological method by which the adherent can attempt to "objectively" impute meaning into his/her life.

But what makes astrology so appealing, though, is that it always refers back to an individual person; it is a thoroughly egotistical affair, wherein the individual finds his/her place in the cosmic order of things. No wonder astrology is so popular despite increasing attacks on its credibility--it talks directly to "me." And when the "I" or "me" is at the forefront of any system, it is always going to find hordes of followers. Perhaps the reason astrology "works" so well is because of our amazing psychological ability to find "meaning" in otherwise meaningless sentences and paragraphs.

A clear example of intention and its ability to extract meaning from almost anything is seen in scriptural readings. Devotees of Islam, Christianity and Sikhism often pose their questions or problems to their respective Holy Books hoping to find a solution. Often the open the work at random and place their fingers on a sentence or paragraph unknowingly but with the keen desire to discover something that speaks to them about their life and work. When they read the selected passage they feel that they have found an appropriate response that pertains directly to their query.

Excluding the possibility of divine intervention, the major factor in this "certainty" of having the "right" answer lies not in the Holy Book itself but in the strong conviction or intention of the devotee. With this tool of intentionality (or intended meaning) one can dig jewels from mud, even if there are no actual jewels to be found. I suggest this is astrology's greatest strength and perhaps the reason for its long survival. I realize that in many ways these discussions are inadequate. To put it in simpler terms, how can one explain a book written supposedly thousands of years ago that pinpoints information about individuals in the future? If deceit or fraud does not provide a complete explanation for this, I think we must agree that an open and unbiased inquiry, which takes the utter profoundness of human consciousness as its starting point, is needed. As I type these sentences the haunting memory of the Bhrigu Samhita's last words to me come to mind, *This young man will come again several times. . . .*

POSTSCRIPT

I suspect that economics, and not the Akashic records on the astral plane, are the driving imperative behind the astrologers' curious leaves.

Not surprisingly, given the unremitting interest in astrology, my article on the Bhrigu Samhita has proven to be the most popular one I have ever written. I have received queries about it from around the world from interested seekers desperate to know how to locate the ancient library. I must confess, though, that I did not write the article as a believer in the book; in fact, I thought so little of its authenticity that I did not write about it for some three years after my trip to India in 1978.

It now appears to me that the book is a fraud. I say this precisely because the work almost invariably mentions how a previous sin (committed in a previous life) can be corrected if someone donates a specific sum of money to the astrologers. Moreover, the astrologers have never "tested" their records scientifically. My hunch now is that something a bit more earthly is happening in Hoshiarpur; the astrologers, I assume, are writing their own horoscopes (with the guidance perhaps of the Bhrigu records) to chart out the lives of those who come to them.

I realize that I do not have proof that the book is a fraud; it is just that in light of Occam's Razor and my own seasoned understanding of Indian astrology I suspect that economics, and not the Akashic records on the astral plane, are the driving imperative behind the astrologers' curious leaves. At this stage what should be done is that a team of qualified specialists visit Hoshiarpur and determine the veracity of the records. Then, and only then, can we know for sure what the Bhrigu Samhita is all about.

Dr. Kary Mullis, Nobel Laureate, **THE ASTROLOGY FILE**

"When I published *Dancing Naked in the Mindfield* there was one eleven page chapter where I mentioned that although astrology had been abandoned by scientific disciplines, it had not been scientifically dispensed with. Meaning, it had not been disproven as a self-consistent set of observations relevant to the human psyche. Not knowing at the time that Gunter Sachs, a Swiss citizen, had published such a study, I offered my own cursory examination from Who's Who in America. When I received a copy of The Astrology File, I was intrigued. Mr. Sachs' book describes a statistical study of a limited but essential part of astrology: where was the sun when you were born, and what do you do for a living. The observation is that something unexplainable, but clearly observable, is going on, to a level of certainty that would be acceptable for a paper in a scientific journal. There is a clear connection, whether you or I like it or not. Gunter Sachs and I became friends as we met together over our mutual interest in astrology, and we decided to undertake an extended study together on this subject."

A major problem facing the study of unidentified flying object sighting reports is the lack of an accurate and comprehensive classification system. What are subsumed under the term "U.F.O.'s" are not merely extraterrestrial spacecrafts but a whole array of psychological, sociological, and even religious phenomena. In order to alleviate the "category errors" inherent in such a diverse field, I have employed the discoveries of Baba Faqir Chand (on the nature of religious visions) and the work of Ken Wilber (in transpersonal psychology) to propose a paradigm from which U.F.O. reports will be studied under three distinct divisions: translative (read: empirical); transformative (read: mental); and transfusive (read: the fusion of empirical and mental modes of knowledge).

With such a tripartite classification system we can begin to view reports of unidentified flying objects in a more understandable light. First, we can distinguish natural occurrences from transmundane apparitions, without damaging the intrinsic quality of the experience itself. Second, though we may continue to search for authentic translative encounters from life forms outside of our own solar system, our main emphasis (in light of transformation) will be to develop a state-of-consciousness-specific understanding of U.F.O.'s. And thirdly, with transfusive experiences -- where transformation and translation intersect -- our investigation will no longer be hampered by the apparent "confusion" of such incidents, but will be able to examine the close link between experiential modes of knowing and empirical-sensory data.

DELHI (JULY 1978)

In July of 1978 I was doing genealogical research at Sawan Ashram in Old Delhi, India. Although I was aptly forewarned that the heat in the summer was excruciating, the ninety percent humidity and one hundred degree plus temperatures overwhelmed me. My only relief from the weather came in the evenings. But even then it was slight.

On the second to last day of my stay, Jean Lyotard, a noted architect from Northern California, and I decided to spend some time on the roof of the monastery. He was leaving in a few days to go back to America. I was to go northward for further research on the Radhasoami tradition. The Indic sky sparkled with stars that night and our conversation eventually turned to astronomy -- the natural extension of which led to the subject of exobiology and UFOs. Jean commented, "I believe UFO's exist and that we have been visited by higher intelligences from other galaxies." Knowing first hand of Jean's intelligence and perceptive observations, I probed further, "Why do you say that?" -- "Because I have seen them myself many times!" His answer was nonchalant. "What were they? Strange lights in the sky, like a luminous ball or a shooting star?" -- "Yes, but more than that. . . I have been contacted by extraterrestrials personally." I gulped, realizing that my dinner of dal and chappatis had not yet been fully digested. "What! come with that again."

"It was in Southern France ten years ago. I was in the countryside when I beheld them. The most beautiful being I have ever seen radiated before me and pointed to the sky. He told me to concentrate on the brilliance above. As I became attentive I was pulled up toward the light. However, the experience was so intense I hesitated and turned away. I have seen them on many occasions. The being was the most exquisite creature. His face, his eyes were. . . well. . . beyond description."

I could not help thinking of several fanciful stories I had read before. Jean's account sounded too much like a headline in *National Enquirer*. But I listened with attention and respect. I appreciated his rationality too much to dismiss his encounter simply as "swamp gas." Jean perceived the alien as a person of advanced spiritual capabilities, distinguishing his visitor from a technological construct. His description had a mystic ring to it, slightly detached from the cold, hardware experiences I had read about happening to Mississippi fishermen and Louisiana housewives. And then, in the midst of our conversation, a remarkable thing occurred. While both of us were taking a momentary glance at the sky, a fine point of light, like a star, caught our attention. Jean immediately recognized it to be a UFO, and predicted what would happen next; "Watch! The light will speed across the sky and will reappear on the opposite side." To my bewilderment, it did exactly that. In its next appearance, which took Jean and I a bit of tracking, he mentioned that it would most likely be joined by another of its kind. And so it was. By this time I was totally absorbed. Four star-like lights streaked across the sky. Maneuvering in an unusual manner, they circled several times in the deep blue vault, disappeared, and came into view distinctly again. Then Jean indicated that the lights would go across the sky once more and reappear. They did.

As the objects manifested, disappeared, and lighted up again in the Asian blackness, I experienced the vividness of a UFO sighting. But the question that remained was one of explanation: satellites? beam reflections? too much curry?

THE HIMALAYAN CONNECTION

Little did I realize that night in Old Delhi that a vital clue to the significance and meaning of UFOs would come a month later when I was doing field work in the foothills of the Himalayas.

Because of my research on the gurus in the Radhasoami tradition, I visited Faqir Chand, a 92-year-old sage who had been engaged in intensive spiritual practices since 1905. He was regarded within the Shabd Yoga community to be one of the most advanced yogic masters in India. It was in Basra Bagdad (Iraq) during World War One when Faqir realized the pivotal secret in understanding transmundane phenomena. The implications for comprehending UFO sightings are staggering. In his autobiography, *The Unknowing Sage*, Faqir relates how in the middle of a battle at Hamidia the form of his guru Shiv Brat Lal manifested to him and said, "Faqir, worry not, the enemy has not come to attack but to take away their dead. Let them do that. Don't waste your ammunition." Faqir then sent for the Subedar Major and narrated the appearance and direction of his guru. He followed the same strategy and all were saved. When Faqir reached Bagdad after the fighting, however, many of Shiv Brat Lal disciples began to worship him instead. Faqir recollected:

"It was all unexpected and strange for me. I enquired of them, "Our Guru Maharaj is at Lahore. I am not your Guru. Why do you worship me?" They replied, "On the battle field, we were in danger. Death lurked in hand. You appeared before us and gave us correct directions. We were spared." I was wonder struck by this explanation. I had no knowledge of it at all. I, myself, being in trouble at that time, had not even remembered them. A mystery shrouded the whole thing, "who appeared inside them?"

When Faqir discovered that his own guru (Shiv Brat Lal) was unaware of his manifestations, he concluded that the answer to the perplexing problem of religious visions must rest in the nature of consciousness itself. Faqir elaborated:

"People say that my Form manifests to them and helps them in solving their worldly as well as mental problems, but I do not go anywhere, nor do I know anything about such miraculous instances. O' Man, your real helper, is your own Self and your own Faith, but you are badly mistaken and believe that somebody from without comes to help you. No Hazrat Mohammed, no Lord Rama, Lord Krishna, or any other Goddess or God comes from without. This entire game is that of your impressions and suggestions which are ingrained upon your mind through your eyes and ears and of your Faith and Belief."

Thus, following Faqir's lucid argument, the modus operandi for religious visions is not due to outside or disconnected forces (although exterior stimuli can act as a catalyst for it), but to the internal process of concentration. A force that for approximately sixteen hours a day enables one to see the everyday, common sense, lawful world, and for another several hours at night can allow one to fly to the moon, converse with unknown people, and create incredible panoramas. Consequently, the appearance and duration of such visions is intimately related to consciousness and focality. Dreaming serves as the classic and perhaps most misunderstood example.

THE CHANDIAN EFFECT

What bearing do the discoveries of the sage of Hoshiarpur have on Jean's experience and those of others like him? Simply this: the nature of one's attention is related directly to the perception one experiences. If our perspective alters so does what we perceive. As ancient Upanishadic speculation and current studies in consciousness have shown, we do not see the world as it "is." Rather, owing to our neurological structures, we see the universe -- incoming stimuli -- relatively; appearances flowing in and out depending on our own biologically defined anatomies. This "predicament" has meaning, content, and purpose within the framework of our own lived-through experiences. However, it is naive to say that our interpretation of life from science, philosophy, or religion absolutely explains the world as it really is. Instead, what we have are metaphorical models of explanation, which work respectively within the brackets of our own purviewed existence. The unseen thread, the larger gestalt, however, will go by undetected. With sharply contoured (mathematical, if you choose) operating mechanisms, we find ourselves living in a universe understood not by pure perception but by alternating analogs.

What these metaphors are (or, more precisely, which level of reality we behold) depends on what I call the *Chandian Effect* -- the experience of certainty, named after the late Faqir Chand who was the first person in the Sant Mat tradition to bring this issue to light. It is from this bedrock quality that we distinguish, acknowledge, and discriminate so-called reality from appearance or illusion. What we call the actual world is dependent solely upon the vibration and consistency in the persuasiveness of certainty. Although we can see, hear, smell, and touch our reality, what determines our conviction that this world is real is not based empirically but is rather an immeasurable quality -- an undefinable feeling. This is strange indeed, for quality is an experience that science cannot study (save as an epiphenomenalism) but without which there would not be any scientific or intellectual endeavors! Science, which is itself rooted primarily upon the concept of materialism (a unified theory of what is real and substantial) excels or disintegrates upon the degree ascertainable of this primordial quality. Hence, quantity -- that which is measurable and which science holds as true and permanent -- proceeds a priori from quality and not vice versa.

Huston Smith has elaborated more on this important distinction: "The experience of certainty is a propelling force behind how we make up our days, fashion our plans, articulate our hopes. If there occurs a break in the Chandian Effect, our normal waking state would collapse into a passing phantasm. Like our nocturnal dreams, it would be stored away and temporarily forgotten. The experience of certainty is so overwhelming that when it radiates forth the question of illusion seldom arises. Just as the chair is quite solid when we strike it with our hand, so too does the world appear concrete and vivid when the Chandian Effect pervades."

Our state of reality is determined by the movement of consciousness into various expressions of the Chandian Effect. Each level of awareness is controlled and empowered by its inherent degree of certainty, which is determined by the intensity and duration of its minimum threshold. Thus, for example, we are predisposed to call the waking state "real" because it is longer (and hence, by extension, more vivid) than the dreaming state. We say this only when we are awake, however, never while we are dreaming. The reason behind this is simple.

At each level where attention is established, a certainty boundary is in effect, which, owing to the given center of awareness, varies in strength, time, and permanence. Hence, even the waking state, although extremely real, only lasts about eighteen hours normally until the Chandian Effect structured upon this level runs down below the minimum threshold and our consciousness shifts to another region. So it is with the dream stage. At the moment of sleep (itself nothing but the transition of attention) we find ourselves occupied in a world that just hours before we thought was nothing but an incredible illusion -- because it was dimmed by the intensity of the certainty force inherent in the waking state -- but with which we now deal quite seriously: running away in terror from death or luring attractive mates for orgasmic satisfaction. From this native pattern of awareness we can see that our lives are simply natural progressions of consciousness from various boundaries within the Chandian Effect. Wilber has detailed this progression, both ontogenetically and phylogenetically, in his transpersonal view of evolution.

THE DEVELOPMENT OF CONSCIOUSNESS

Wilber illustrates in his book *The Atman Project* (1980) that consciousness develops essentially along two major avenues: translation and transformation. When attention gravitates within a given state (e.g. the waking state), neither altering it nor transcending it, translation ensues. Awareness is thus established within a particular field of the Chandian Effect, being held in constriction by the inherent certainty boundary. This does not mean, however, that change is not taking place -- it indeed is -- but only that the change is within given parameters. In other words, although there is a constant flux in our waking world, the changes themselves do not radically convert the state itself. Smith describes this same movement of attention as horizontal, development that proceeds along (i.e. within) the given plane of action.

On the other side, the shift of consciousness from one state to another (Wilber points out clearly that it can both ascend and descend), or the conversion of the realm itself, is called transformative. In this regard an entirely different state of awareness is experienced. It is an ontologically diverse expression of the Chandian Effect with a new certainty boundary and threshold. Smith calls it vertical ascension, and religiously it is known as ganz andere, the mysterium tremendum.

In twentieth century western civilization, with its persistent materialism and psychological reductionism (aspects of translation), anything which is exterior to the translative world must be reduced down to a simpler, and thus graspable, component. If the transformative event cannot be collapsed, which Wilber, Smith, and others argue that it cannot, it may be classified as a "hallucination" -- which explains nothing. Or, the "ganz andere" experience may be elevated to the unapproachable ideal, goal, or god of the culture. Wilber explicitly details the difference between translation and transformation:

"It comes to the same thing to say that translation is a change in surface structures, and transformation is a change in deep structures. Recall our simple analogy of an eight-story building; each of its floors is a deep structure, while all the particular objects (rooms, furniture, offices, etc.) on each floor are its surface structures. Translation, then, is moving around on one floor; transformation is moving to a different floor altogether."

A third aspect to the development of consciousness that Wilber briefly touched upon in *Up From Eden* but did not define concisely is what I call transfusion, the intersecting of translation with transformation. Often when consciousness proceeds to a higher level it does not do so wholly, remaining partially within the lower order. It is, therefore, difficult to determine what is genuinely transformative from a radical translative event. And this situation is especially compounded when both forms of development are taking place simultaneously. With a reductionist paradigm we presume that the higher comes from the lower (where in actuality the opposite is true; Smith, 1976) and thus tend to misread transformation as an aberration on the real (read: translative) world. This concept of transfusion, which is why there exists so much confusion in the field, is important in understanding how consciousness can at one end transform and on the other translate but at the same instant not be mutually exclusive.

It should also be added that mistaking the higher with the lower can also work in reverse. For instance, certain religious experiences that appear nonrational are sometimes elevated to a transrational status, when, in fact, they are prerational.

Transfusion can work in both directions, thereby causing scholars to commit what Wilber calls a pre/trans fallacy. Materialistic science has a tendency to reduce higher modes of being, whereas uncritical transpersonal psychologists have a proclivity to categorize nonrational experiences as transmundane. Both lack a clear and incisive structuralism according to Wilber.

TOWARD A TRIPARTITE CLASSIFICATION SYSTEM OF UFO REPORTS

This leads us to the main thesis of this article: a tripartite classification system of unidentified flying object sighting reports. Employing the preceding terminology on the development of consciousness, we can place experiences of UFOs within three major categories: translative, transformative, and transfusive.

Translation (Fusion: Empirically Verifiable)

Simply put, translative experiences of UFOs are perceptions of natural phenomena within the consensus reality that have yet to be named or identified correctly. For the most part, UFO researchers have been trying to prove the empirical (that is, scientifically verifiable) basis behind unidentified flying objects. This is, above all else, primarily a translative endeavor, attempting to place UFOs within a rational and, therefore, explainable paradigm. However, there is a major problem confronting this attempt. The term UFO has become synonymous with alien creatures or spaceships that have come from other planets or galaxies. The near impossibility of such visits by extraterrestrials has been pointed out by several eminent scientists, including Carl Sagan. Besides the evidence being scant (or nonexistent), the explanations for "close encounters" or sightings do not necessarily have to be exobiological or exotechnological; in fact, as Vallee indicates, they could well be sociological.

Thus, it is likely that most of what we call unidentified flying objects are nothing more than satellites, "falling stars" (meteorites), weather balloons, disguised defense operations and a whole array of natural phenomena. Nevertheless, translative investigations conceivably could encounter extraterrestrials and place their findings before the general public as long as there was empirical data sufficient to support such an event.

Transformation (Diffusion: Experientially Verifiable Through Consciousness)

Among the millions of UFO sightings reported each year, there are a select few that describe vivid and remarkable personal encounters with extraterrestrial beings. No matter what rational (i.e., translative) explanations may be offered to account for this type of experience, the contactee while undergoing the event will perceive it as extremely real (and, in some cases, more real than our own waking world) and will be convinced of its authenticity. Science generally will not be able to grasp this experience in itself and will classify it as an "hallucination", as some scientists have done with Near-Death Experiences, or, if following Carl Sagan's lead, "a miswiring in human neuroanatomy." Although these may look like plausible explanations for such transmundane phenomena, they do not in essence explain the occurrences "as is." Rather, they reduce the experiences down to fit an empirical-sensory model. This reductionism is particularly misleading and, if allowed to dominate our thinking, reduces higher, more unified modes of being.

An example of the basic flaw in this outlook is language. To understand the novel, *The Great Gatsby*, for instance, the whole story must be read. It is on that level alone that the intention of the writer is most completely apprehended. Now you can break the work down to its chapter headings, and then to its paragraph arrangement, then to its sentence structure, and finally to its words. Yet if you were only to examine the letters themselves, not the words they make up, nor the sentences they form, nor the entire paragraphs they construct, and finally the story they compose, then the entire point, intention, and purpose of the novel is lost. Reductionism is often anti-informational and does not increase our understanding but only constricts it. Wilber elaborates:

"The truth of the naturic realm is decided by empirical (sensory) data, but the truth of the mental realm. . . is established only by intersubjective discussion among a community of concerned interpreters, whose data is not sensory but symbolic. The point is that even though truths in the mental-symbolic sphere are non-empirical and cannot be determined by empiric-scientific inquiry, nontheless they can be decided. . . I consider exclusive empiricism to be radically and violently reductionistic, no matter how cleverly concealed; the demand for "empirical proof" is really a demand to strip the higher levels of being of their meaning and value and present them only in their aspects that can be reduced to objective, sensory, value-free univalent dimensions."

Thus, following Wilber's argument, there can be transformative UFO encounters that are symbols emerging from a separate ontological ground of consciousness. Some may argue about why there isn't any physical (empirical) proof for such a novel and important event. Just as a dreamer cannot bring the actual "substance" of his or her dream into the waking world, but only its symbols, and just as the materialist cannot carry his or her universe into a dream (except symbolically), so too is it for the UFO contactee who experiences a transformative incident.

Transfusion [Confusion: The Intersection of Translation with Transformation]

The third and last category represents the intersecting of translation with transformation which I have termed transfusion. Perhaps the reason why many UFO reports are so fantastically mixed up, irrational, or weird is because of the fusion of these two forms of development. A good example of this was presented on the ABC news show 20/20. In an attempt to explain how one young man had a close encounter of the third kind, it was shown that at the moment of his experience an underground vault emitted electrical currents of light that formed strange apparitions in the sky. When that same light struck the young man it may have invoked a temporary alteration in his brain and thus produced an hallucination (later recounted as a "UFO abduction"). Viewers of the television program, after hearing two scientists give rational (i.e., translative) explanations for apparent UFO landings, may have become convinced that what the man witnessed was a natural, if uncommon, occurrence. However, the contactee himself, because he underwent a transformative experience (seeing it as real and as objective as the print on this page), could not really accept the translative natural explanation. This confusion of many UFO encounters accounts for why the subject is riddled with fanaticism, religiosity, and garbled hokum.

It should be remembered, however, that simply because a UFO contact is nonrational does not mean that it is necessarily a transrational experience. As Wilber has shown about dreams the same applies to UFO encounters. Psychologists and UFO-ologists must distinguish between prerational states (which, in Wilber's terminology, includes the archaic-uroboric, magical-typhonic, and the mythic-membership stages) and transrational states (which encompasses psychic, subtle and causal structures; Wilber, 1981a).

In light of transfusion, what may be occurring in several UFO encounters is a regression from rationality into subconscious and prepersonal states. Such relapses may be triggered, though, by physiological or translative elements. Carl Jung, for instance, argues along this line in his book

, pointing out that many UFO sighting reports have the earmarks of being archetypes projected into consciousness by the Collective Unconscious. However, because Jung is not clear in distinguishing between prerational and transrational archetypes (he usually fuses the two; Wilber, 1982b), he fails to differentiate between regressive and progressive UFO encounters. Nevertheless, the important point in all of this is that we investigate all nonrational experiences with a critical structuralism and an empathetic phenomenological hermeneutics.

CONCLUSION

With the classification system I have proposed we can begin to view reported experiences of UFOs in a nonreductionistic and more understandable light (see Table 1). First, we can distinguish natural occurrences from transmundane apparition, without damaging the intrinsic quality of the experience itself. Second, though we may continue to search for authentic translative encounters from life forms outside of our own solar system, our main emphasis (in light of transformation) will be to develop a state-of-consciousness-specific understanding of UFOs. And thirdly, with transfusive experiences -- where translation and transformation intersect -- our investigation will no longer be hampered by the apparent confusion of such incidents, but will be able to examine the close link between experiential modes of knowing and empirical sensory data.

Hence, what I am arguing for in the field of UFO studies is the same thing that Ken Wilber in *A Sociable God* argues for in the study of religious phenomena: a hierarchical structuralism. Because UFOs are not merely extraterrestrial spacecraft, but a whole array of psychological, sociological, and even religious phenomena, a "transcendental sociology" is needed in order that UFO studies does not fall prey to materialistic reductionism or uncritical phenomenological hermeneutics.

Indeed, such a transpersonal structuralism is concordant with the Chandian Effect. When the certainty boundary is questioned intensively, or naturally transcended, the attractive and binding force of that level of consciousness recedes, revealing the tentative nature of its existence. As Wilber has clearly indicated there is an ascendant ontology behind the evolution of the universe, one which is marked by an increasing degree of awareness. This idea must be kept in the forefront of UFO-ologists' minds, because unidentified flying objects are more than a exotechnological issue.

By applying the tripartite paradigm that I have proposed (which will, of course, become more sophisticated and exact in time) it will serve as a critical normative to the UFO phenomena, allowing for a much needed structural adjudication. For instance, in looking back at my experiences atop Sawan Ashram in Old Delhi, India, it would appear that what I experienced was not remarkably *ganz andere*, but was most likely a peculiar translative event with naturalistic explanations. However, what Jean Lyotard witnessed in Southern France, or what Faqir Chand saw in Basra Bagdad, was of a transformative dimension, in that a higher state of awareness was experienced.

The real mystery, therefore, is not in alien space creatures who prey upon naive inhabitants, but in the very nature of attention. To comprehend the restraining certainty hold of the Chandian Effect and how consciousness evolves through its various boundary thresholds is the most important frontier awaiting the study of UFOs. The problem, as several UFO-ologists have already stated, has not been a case of "unidentified" but one of "misidentified".

POSTSCRIPT

The overwhelming evidence suggests that we have yet to be visited by E.T.'s.

Although I still hold that the tripartite schema via Wilber and Chand is useful when studying unidentified flying objects, it has become clearer to me -- especially after hundreds of individuals now claim to have sightings of Elvis -- that cultural values and needs plays a huge part in any kind of religious (quasi or otherwise) phenomenon. True we should still be open to the faint possibility that there may be some kind of alien contact in the future, but the overwhelming evidence suggests that we have yet to be visited by E.T.'s. It seems far more likely that what we classify as close encounters of the third or fourth kind are really misidentified projectiles of our own psycho-social biography. What is truly impressive in all of this, of course, is the mind's ability to adapt to new cultural trends with such religious zeal. The power behind all of this is the brain's own chemistry which gives such tremendous hardware (conviction, if you will) to the wide variance of religious or cultural ideas. Such ideas may not be real in any ontological sense of the term, but they nevertheless "feel" real because of the brain's amazing plasticity and ability to energize whatever it is conned into believing. Thus the current rage in U.F.O.'s says much more about our almost infinite desire to believe in almost anything (regardless of truth, facticity, or common sense) than it does about some significant exo-biological invasion from Sirius.

5 | Gumby Land

In the Fall of 1981 while I was teaching at Chaminade College Preparatory, a Catholic High School in the San Fernando Valley, Gumby fever had taken hold of hundreds of students who couldn't get enough of Art Clokey's Claymation creation.

So when it was announced in the local newspapers that Art Clokey was going to attend a Gumby film festival in Santa Monica (barely 30 minutes away), a number of Chaminade students and myself made the pilgrimage.

We were not disappointed as the theatre was packed and some classic Gumby and Pokey cartoons from the past were shown with all their bendable glory.

However, something very odd occurred at the end of the show. Instead of a Gumby montage or a Pokey homage, we saw a film of Sathya Sai Baba, the famous guru from India, performing what appeared to be some sort of divine miracle as he was pulling enormous amounts of ash out of a small vase. It was an impressive sequence, even if a bizarrely juxtaposed one. None of the students knew what to make of it since they had never heard of Sai Baba nor seen any of his alleged divine manifestations.

Art Clokey then came on stage to explain what we had just seen. He told us that he had gone through a rough patch in his life and decided to go to India on a spiritual journey. He took Gumby with him and, accordingly, when he met the famed Sathya Sai Baba, the master magically produced vibhutti (sacred ash) and directly spread it over Gumby, declaring that "Gumby was the incarnation of spiritual love."

Shortly thereafter, Art Clokey claims that his life turned around and that Gumby toy sales increased. As the Gumby and Pokey Claymation website explains it,

"Clokey remarried in 1976 and three years later, he and his new wife Gloria traveled to Bangalore, India to visit a guru named Sathya Sai Baba who supposedly had amazingly magical powers. For some reason, Clokey brought a Gumby doll along to their audience with the guru. 'I stood there with Gumby and he did this circular motion with his arms,' Clokey says. 'Out of nowhere he materialized this sacred ash. He plopped it right on top of Gumby. When we came home again, things started to happen.' Gumby toy sales began to pick up, and then Eddie

Murphy started doing a continuing Gumby skit on Saturday Night Live. Suddenly, the phone started ringing and Gumby was hip again. Clokey went on a lecture tour and received an $8 million contract with Lorimar for a new Gumby series. He started work on Gumby—the Movie.' Gumby is a symbol of the spark of divinity in each of us, the basis of the ultimate value of each person. Eddie Murphy instinctively picked up on this when he asserted, 'I'm Gumby, dammit!' wrote Clokey in 1986. 'When people watch Gumby, they get a blissful feeling. Gumby loves you. We love you. That's about all I can say.'"

Later on when I was talking to a Sathya Sai Baba devotee from India I was informed that a tiny shrine was created for Gumby who was worshipped as a divine icon and some spiritual aspirants performed puja to his image in the belief that Gumby was given special powers to help one in their meditation and sadhana.

Of course, whenever I retell this incredulous tale to my college students they invariably laugh as if it was the most absurd thing they have ever heard. But then I remind them that almost all religious claims sound odd from an outsider's perspective, whether it be a virgin birth, transubstantiation, or extraterrestrial beings imprisoned around volcanoes 75 million years ago. Yet, in most of these cases the common denominator is that they involve something paranormal, metaphysical, or transcendent. The problem, though, with such claims is that they tend not to be testable since they are more often than not predicated upon faith and belief and not necessarily on evidence or proof. This isn't surprising since most devotees are not attempting to scientifically validate their respective beliefs.

I bring up the subject of Gumby and the spiritual claims surrounding him because I am often asked in class about the verdicality of certain metaphysical claims that abound in religious mythologies. My usual rejoinder is that we don't want to enter into "Gumby Land" when doing philosophy, since most of these kinds of questions (how many angels can sit atop an empty coke bottle?) are literally *nonsense* (in the precise definition of that term as first coined in the 17th century).

The Gumby Land Mantra: "You are not even wrong!"

Wolfgang Pauli, the noted physicist who won a Nobel Prize for his work in subatomic physics, is credited with the famous German witticism, "*Das ist nicht nur nicht richtig, es ist nicht einmal falsch!*" which translates in English as "Not only is it not right, it's not even wrong!"

Pauli's acerbic comment, apparently directed at an exceptionally unclear physics paper he had received for review from a young budding scientist, has been widely cited as a shorthand version of Karl Popper's principle of falsifiability in science. Essentially, any hypothesis or theory must be open to experimental confirmation or refutation. If such an idea cannot be falsified then it remains in the realm of speculation. In other words, while we may postulate any host of theories about why such and such works this way or that (using our imagination to the fullest), if we wish to gain scientific credibility we must rationally and empirically test our claims in this world. The reason science has made such enormous progress is precisely because it tests its claims and allows for a record of successes and failures, always realizing that our knowledge is tentative and open for revision. Undoubtedly there are several areas in science, such as string theory, which provide rich possibilities (coupled with some remarkable mathematical breakthroughs) that have yet to be properly tested, but even here scientists agree that progress can only be made if and when differing hypotheses can be rigorously verified.

However, some religious claims seem, at least on the surface, to be resistant to such testing or, even worse, so muddled and abstract that they cannot offer a pathway in which they can be verified positively or negatively. It is this latter quality (which to be fair is also rampant in almost all human affairs, including science) to which Wolfgang's terse criticism of "not even wrong" is most aptly applied.

W.V. Quine, the well-known mathematician and philosopher from Harvard, once quipped, "Theories face the tribunal of experience as a whole." Put differently, science is the process by which alternative theories and ideas compete against each other in the empirical and rational world and in an almost Darwinian fashion (caveats do exist here, as any sociologist of knowledge will warn us) where the winner is the one who can survive the gauntlet of repudiations. Naturally, the theoretic battles never cease and even the most lauded of winners (from Newton's theory of gravity to Einstein's theory of relativity) are constantly facing new challenges and modifications, even if they retain some sort of familial resemblance from their earlier ancestral forms.

I have in my academic career come across a plethora of Gumby Land (Pauli's "not even wrong") examples in the borderland areas of religion and mysticism which wish to be regarded as viable science but which on closer inspection turn out to be anything but.

One of the more recent and virulent illustrations of Gumby Land thinking comes from Ken Wilber, the popular New Age theorist, who both in print and in a series of audio lectures/interviews has claimed that love and creativity is what drove the big bang and which to this day is the driving force behind life and evolution. While it may be understandable to say such things as a religious or emotional expression, Wilber goes much further and alleges that there is a genuine scientific aspect to his loved filled creationism. Frank Visser, myself, and others have in a series of articles heavily criticized Wilber over his misunderstanding of evolutionary biology, but the real underlying problem with Wilber's intelligent design postulations is that due to their extreme generalizations and mythological layering they cannot be falsified in any meaningful way. In point of fact, Wilber has a long track record of not even properly considering reasoned criticisms of his position and has tended to engage in long rants about how "on top of the latest research" he is, forgetting in the process that it isn't about him but his theories that generate such heated disagreement. Wilber doesn't have empirical support for his "it is all love" hypothesis about the Big Bang and the like. He has his beliefs on the subject, no doubt, but his integral theory about the creation of the known and unknown worlds is pure Gumby Land and as such qualifies under the Pauli banner of "not even wrong."

This doesn't mean that Wilber couldn't refine his creationist musings and posit some viable hypotheses that could indeed be tested and thus qualify under this "could be wrong" rubric. But in order to do that Wilber would have to focus more time on generating falsifiable experiments that don't merely rely on castigating fellow skeptics with such muddled banter as, "But I suppose it should be pointed out that many of the ideas these critics offer are in fact at a green or orange altitude, and not even teal or turquoise altitude...." Wilber's descent into color-coding his critics is, as some commentators have already pointed out, a new form of intellectual racism. Instead of debating the nuanced merits of an argument (which takes time and patience) Wilber has, ironically, developed a reductionistic (and somewhat absurdist) methodology whereby both the critic and his/her criticism is a priori relegated to a questionable rung in his Integral ladder.

Wilber also indulges in a series of sleight of hand statistics that are part and parcel of his Gumby Land leanings. For instance, Wilber writes, "Integral Institute is a sanctuary for second- and third-tier consciousness. And this means, a sanctuary for anybody who can rise to their own highest potential. That 2% really means the highest 2% of your very own being. Absolutely every single person is capable of rising to their own second-tier awareness (and third tier as well in this Great Liberation), rising to their own greatness, and that is what I-I is all about, rising to your own highest 2%, your own highest Self, and meeting there your own extraordinary greatness. Do you want to be part of the herd, or part of your own greatness? Every single one of you can rise to your own genius, every single one of you can do this... "

Again, such rhetoric is often employed in business advertisements when attempting to win new consumers, but as such it hardly qualifies as something that is truly quantifiable. How does one go around testing to see which is or isn't the "2% of your highest Self"?

Or, in another context, Wilber employs another questionable statistic, "Run the numbers. Even if we say there were only one billion Chinese over the course of its history (an extremely low estimate), that still means that only one thousand out of one billion had graduated into an authentic, transformative spirituality. For those of you without a calculator, that's 0.0000001 of the total population. And that means, unmistakably, that the rest of the population were (and are) involved in, at best, various types of horizontal, translative, merely legitimate religion: they were involved in magical practices, mythical beliefs, egoic petitionary prayer, magical rituals, and so on-in other words, translative ways to give meaning to the separate self, a translative function that was, as we were saying, the major social glue of the Chinese (and all other) cultures to date."

While I might understand a preacher using such numbers hyperbolically to rouse his congregation, what doesn't quite compute is how Wilber derives such exacting numbers in the first place. Are we really supposed to derive statistical extrapolations about the spiritual state of billions of sentiment human beings on the planet earth because of two Zen master interviews that Ken Wilber has conducted? Is this a testable claim or just a hyped form of misusing math to win new converts?

Of course, given this kind of methodological anarchy, where numbers and colors intertwine under the pretense of "integral" science, then maybe worshipping Gumby makes more sense than we realize. Or, perhaps not even being wrong is what we get when we confuse our mystical endeavors with objectivist science.

This leads us to the inherent difficulty in absolutely disproving metaphysical propositions since we do not have access to such rarified realms if they do indeed exist. For instance, it may well be true that Gumby and Pokey are divine beings who are dispensing untold blessings from their astral habitat, but we have no way of confirming beyond any reasonable doubt that such is the case. Just as we cannot disprove that karma and reincarnation are really morally operative or that original sin is why human beings suffer and die. Simply put, when it comes to the transcendent we can postulate any sort of nonsense that we wish and rest assured that it cannot be wholly disproven. Gumby Land, in other words, offers us an infinite set of possibilities--the vast lot of which can neither be tested nor proven.

Bertrand Russell, one of the great polymaths of the 20th century, captured the fallaciousness of this sort of reasoning when he opined in 1952 in an unpublished essay, "Many orthodox people speak as though it were the business of sceptics to disprove received dogmas rather than of dogmatists to prove them. This is, of course, a mistake. If I were to suggest that between the Earth and Mars there is a china teapot revolving about the sun in an elliptical orbit, nobody would be able to disprove my assertion provided I were careful to add that the teapot is too small to be revealed even by our most powerful telescopes. But if I were to go on to say that, since my assertion cannot be disproved, it is intolerable presumption on the part of human reason to doubt it, I should rightly be thought to be talking nonsense. If, however, the existence of such a teapot were affirmed in ancient books, taught as the sacred truth every Sunday, and instilled into the minds of children at school, hesitation to believe in its existence would become a mark of eccentricity and entitle the doubter to the attentions of the psychiatrist in an enlightened age or of the Inquisitor in an earlier time."

Six years later, Russell elaborated, "I ought to call myself an agnostic; but, for all practical purposes, I am an atheist. I do not think the existence of the Christian God any more probable than the existence of the Gods of Olympus or Valhalla. To take another illustration: nobody can prove that there is not between the Earth and Mars a china teapot revolving in an elliptical orbit, but nobody thinks this sufficiently likely to be taken into account in practice. I think the Christian God just as unlikely."

Russell's argument on closer inspection is a pragmatic one (since, given his example, it may indeed be possible one day to find out if there is a china pot revolving in an elliptical orbit between Earth and Mars) and underlines how much of science is a practical and common sense approach to unraveling the complicated workings of the cosmos at large. Yet, the pathways to such unravelings are often counter intuitive and in some instances defy our common sensibilities. This was brought into sharp focus with the development of quantum mechanics during the 1920s and 1930s. Nevertheless, science's ultimate successes are precisely when it can proffer experimental evidences and/or testable predictions for its theories. If science cannot do that, then it remains in the impasse zone, like string theory, where it can only offer promissory notes but no cash in hand.

Because of the plasticity of human consciousness we have the wonderful ability to virtually simulate all sorts of fantastic adventures and, undoubtedly, this vast imaginative capacity has greatly improved our survival chances in a world of competing animals, instincts, and options. But when we ground such musings in this empirical arena and overlay them with what the world portends and offers up we oftentimes find that our maps have gaps. It is when those gaps are acknowledged that progress can be made since then and only then can we tinker and improve upon our limited knowledge systems.

To better understand the progressive differences between science and religion all one has to do is ponder how often a holy book changes over time and compare it to how often a chemistry or biological textbook gets altered or modified. Where the former may change very little, if at all after a set period of time (e.g., the *Quran*, the *New Testament*, the *Guru Granth Sahib*), the latter is under immense pressures (from an array of new research and findings) to update its data and discoveries year-to-year, if not month-to-month. Arguably, the stark contrasts between religion and science can be best summarized by looking at how willing each of them are to admit to being wrong and how transparent they are in providing such admissions, particularly with regard to core doctrines or theories.

Invariably I have a student in one of my college courses on science and religion who wishes to propose a metaphysical explanation for a naturalistic event, whether it is a new stylized version of creationism or a subtler than quanta interpretation of disease. My rejoinder is that in order to do science properly (even if we allow for the wildest of speculations at first) we have to ultimately find ways to verify our proposals in the sensible world. If we fail to do such, then we are literally in Gumby Land where belief and faith hold sway (and imaginary beings hold court), but where doubt and reason are regarded as unwelcome enemies trying to undermine the unchecked fantasies of a brain designed to conjure up all sorts of nonsense in its virtual simulations--simulations which if held too firmly mislead us into an illusory conflation of what may truly be correlative or even causative with what is merely the remnant exhaust of an excited cerebral hemisphere too addicted to its own dopamine to grasp the simplest of observations.

The most fundamental of observations for which science is constantly reminding us anew is that what we think to be true may not be so and therefore inviting other minds to participate and cross check what we observe can lead to all sorts of unexpected results, ranging from the discoveries of new planets to new medicines. But in order to allow for a participatory understanding of the universe (and not merely our solipsistic version of it) we are required to do that most radical of things: we must be willing to confess our own ignorance and be willing to follow the lines of evidence wherever it my lead us, even if in its sojourn it upturns our previously held cherished ideas or truths.

As Richard Feynman, one of the chief architects behind Quantum Electrodynamics, once illuminated, "It is in the admission of ignorance and the admission of uncertainty that there is a hope for the continuous motion of human beings in some direction that doesn't get confined, permanently blocked, as it has so many times before in various periods in the history of man."

And perhaps, in light of Feynman's elucidations, we unearth that the real danger of Gumby Land is that instead of liberating our thinking and setting our sails off to vast uncharted waters, it can curtail our understanding of reality by not demanding enough of our premonitions and our musings. Nature's selective process demands, even if we are not up to the task, that we be tested time and time again to see if we can survive its unending gauntlets. So too does science demand that our guesses and theories be vetted lest we succumb to a premature and smug acceptance of our own narcissistic predilections. Our task is as Feynman stressed "to try to give all the information to help others to judge the value of your contribution; not just the information that leads to judgment in one particular direction or another." Additionally, Feynman's most famous dictum reminds us of an often-ignored truism,

> *"That you must not fool yourself and you are the easiest person to fool."*

Feynman on the Scientific Method

"It's a kind of scientific integrity, a principle of scientific thought that corresponds to a kind of utter honesty—a kind of leaning over backwards. For example, if you're doing an experiment, you should report everything that you think might make it invalid—not only what you think is right about it: other causes that could possibly explain your results; and things you thought of that you've eliminated by some other experiment, and how they worked—to make sure the other fellow can tell they have been eliminated.

Details that could throw doubt on your interpretation must be given, if you know them. You must do the best you can—if you know anything at all wrong, or possibly wrong—to explain it. If you make a theory, for example, and advertise it, or put it out, then you must also put down all the facts that disagree with it, as well as those that agree with it. There is also a subtler problem. When you have put a lot of ideas together to make an elaborate theory, you want to make sure, when explaining what it fits, that those things it fits are not just the things that gave you the idea for the theory; but that the finished theory makes something else come out right, in addition. In summary, the idea is to try to give all of the information to help others to judge the value of your contribution; not just the information that leads to judgment in one particular direction or another. A great deal of their difficulty is, of course, the difficulty of the subject and the inapplicability of the scientific method to the subject....

We have learned a lot from experience about how to handle some of the ways we fool ourselves. One example: Millikan measured the charge on an electron by an experiment with falling oil drops, and got an answer which we now know not to be quite right. It's a little bit off, because he had the incorrect value for the viscosity of air. It's interesting to look at the history of measurements of the charge of the electron, after Millikan. If you plot them as a function of time, you find that one is a little bigger than Millikan's, and the next one's a little bit bigger than that, and the next one's a little bit bigger than that, until finally they settle down to a number which is higher. Why didn't they discover that the new number was higher right away? It's a thing that scientists are ashamed of—this history-because it's apparent that people did things like this: When they got a number that was too high above Millikan's, they thought something must be wrong—and they would look for and find a reason why something might be wrong. When they got a number closer to Millikan's value they didn't look so hard. And so they eliminated the numbers that were too far off, and did other things like that. We've learned those tricks nowadays, and now we don't have that kind of a disease.

But this long history of learning how not to fool ourselves—of having utter scientific integrity—is, I'm sorry to say, something that we haven't specifically included in any particular course that I know of. We just hope you've caught on by osmosis. The first principle is that you must not fool yourself—and you are the easiest person to fool. So you have to be very careful about that. After you've not fooled yourself, it's easy not to fool other scientists. You just have to be honest in a conventional way after that."

6 | *The Shadow of a God Man*

I first heard of Sathya Sai Baba when I was 15 years old. We were on a family summer vacation in Idyllwild, California, and on one lazy afternoon I walked into the local library which was then situated in Fern Valley a short distance away from our cabin. I picked up a book by Arnold Schulman simply titled *Baba*, which described in colorful details the miraculous exploits of Sathya Sai Baba, who had become renowned throughout India for both his extraordinary powers and for his teachings on love. Although I enjoyed the narrative immensely, I felt even then that something rang false about Schulman's narrative. Simply put, Sai Baba's miracles looked suspiciously like magic tricks. Years later, my gut reaction turned out to be correct, as overwhelming photographic evidence emerged which indeed demonstrated that Sai Baba faked his miracles by doing some very amateurish magic tricks—tricks, by the way, that even a child could reproduce given enough practice.

In the 1980s, Brian Walsh and I founded a journal called *Understanding Cults and Spiritual Movements* (UCSM) which was designed to critically analyze a number of gurus and masters in America, Europe, and India. In the second to last issue of that journal, I wrote a review of an affirmative Sai Baba book entitled *My Baba and I*, which was written by Jack Hislop, who at the time was the President of the North American Sai Baba organization. While I enjoyed the book, I found some of Hislop's claims to be deeply questionable. Jack Hislop didn't take too much offense at my pointed review and we began a friendly correspondence that lasted over a year or so. Ultimately, this led to a serious discussion on whether or not Sathya Sai Baba had actually raised one of his disciples, Walter Cowan, from the dead. Since Hislop was very close to Sathya Sai Baba at that time, he served more or less as a vocal spokesperson for Sai Baba who claimed that he actually did raise Walter Cowan, a former Kirpal Singh initiate and group representative, from the dead.

In the early 1990s, I created a website called *The Neural Surfer*. Several sections of that website were devoted to shedding light on the hidden exploits of a number of nefarious spiritual leaders, including Thakar Singh, John-Roger Hinkins, and Sathya Sai Baba. Eventually, a number of devotees of Sai Baba contacted me about how they were duped by their guru, primarily because they felt they had been sexually exploited by their leader under false pretenses. Several of these devotees described in vivid detail about how Sai Baba had sexually seduced them. After these reports appeared on my website, I started getting attacked from various Sai factions worldwide, which eventually led to letters being written to UCSD and MSAC demanding that my website be taken off the internet. In addition, several websites were created attempting to cast doubts on Sai's sexual exploits as well as attacking the veracity of my research on him and the integrity of those who claimed abuse. One very highly placed politician in India contacted UCSD about my website and I was politely asked by the Webmaster at UCSD to take down my site to avoid further political turmoil. I then transferred my site to MSAC, but even here the President of the college was asked to shut down The *Neural Surfer*. Thankfully, the President of the college refused to do so on the grounds of academic freedom.

Because of this, I felt it would be important to create an open discussion forum on Yahoo groups where interested participants could voice their experiences and opinions (positively or negatively) on Sai Baba. For many years this became a focal point for airing many grievances about Sathya Sai Baba, particularly his sexual relations with a number of disciples from around the world. Unfortunately, however, it also became a haven for a tremendous amount of spam-generated posting. I also started to receive a number of disturbing personal threats from varying quarters because I was the founder of the forum. Finally, I had to shut down the group due to these continuing and unrelenting threats.

In 1999/2000 I was contacted by a couple of highly placed Sai Baba devotees who wanted to present their "findings" to the world about the hidden side of Sai Baba. We had discussions about putting their material on my website and other portals. Eventually, they decided to create a separate site singularly devoted to the manipulative exploits of India's most famous guru. Their findings caused a worldwide uproar in the Sai Baba community and led to the cover story in *India Today* about Sai Baba's exploits. BBC even commissioned a documentary entitled The Secret Swami which went into lurid detail about the guru's hidden life.

The following articles, which date back to the late 1980s, provide a glimpse into some of the controversies surrounding Sathya Sai Baba during his lifetime.

MY BABA AND I BY JOHN S. HISLOP: A BOOK REVIEW

Dr. John S. Hislop is a remarkable person: intelligent, well-read, extremely open-minded, and a seasoned spiritual seeker. Thus, it is difficult not to be impressed with his personal account of his relationship with the renowned Avatar Sathya Sai Baba of India. It is an easy reading book, filled with fascinating vignettes of Sathya Sai Baba's alleged miraculous powers and intense love for his devotees.

However, there is a major problem with the book: the supposed evidence Hislop cites in support of Sai Baba's miracles (like materializing objects from thin air) has not been scientifically examined or tested. For instance, how do we know that Sathya Sai Baba is nothing more than a clever magician (as D. Scott Rogo, Amazing Randi, and others suggest)? Why doesn't Sai Baba materialize an object that is so totally beyond physical manipulation that even materialistic scientists would concede to its miraculous origins? Put bluntly, Sai Baba produces religious trinkets; he has never produced a billion dollars—money which could be used for thousands of starving Indians.

Why not? If we apply the principle of Occam's Razor and the suggestive accounts of Tal Brooke (author of the very controversial, *Lord Of The Air*) the answer is fairly obvious: Sai Baba is not a man of miracles, he is a man of shrewd magic tricks. Now there is nothing wrong with a magician preaching love for God, but there is something reprehensible about a stage artist claiming his sleight of hand tricks are Divinely ordained. Hislop writes at length about the most extraordinary object Sathya Sai Baba has ever created for the joy of his devotees—a small cross with a miniaturized figure of Jesus Christ. According to Hislop, the object was constructed from the actual cross Jesus was nailed to. Sai Baba reconstituted the material from its disintegrated molecular parts. An incredible tale, no doubt, but where's the proof? The cross has never been thoroughly scrutinized by a team of qualified scientists. Moreover, even a cursory look at the cross (a photograph of it appears in Hislop's book) does not suggest a Divine origin; it looks like any other religious trinket—except that it is unusually small. The replication also has a major historical flaw in it as it depicts Jesus with nails in the palms of his hands. History tells us that people crucified in Jesus' time had nails driven in their wrists not their palms. Yet, despite the evidence to the contrary, Hislop waxes in

59

eloquent prose about Sathya Sai Baba's amazing manifestations, forgetting in the process that "Amazing Randi"—the noted paranormal debunker—can also perform the same "miracles" Sathya Sai Baba can, although he does not claim Divine intervention.

This is not to suggest that Sathya Sai Baba doesn't have good things to say about spirituality (he does), but only that there is no positive proof whatsoever to substantiate Sai Baba's Avatar status, except for the (scientifically) untested faith and testimony of his earnest devotees. I personally welcome the day when Sai Baba performs his miracles under scientifically controlled circumstances; then, and only then, can we make some rational pronouncements about his divine powers.

JACK HISLOP CORRESPONDENCE

Dear David:

Thanks indeed for the current issue of your journal which is just now forwarded to me by my Birth Day Publishing Co., and for the kind words about the book, *My Baba and I*, and its author. From the writing to the editing to the printing to the expensive paper, your journal is a quality product and as such is aimed at and no doubt reaches influential people. You are certainly an intellectual man with a long background of sound, hard practical experience, and yourself and the people who read your words are most important in society because you are opinion makers, and your firm opinions influence the attitudes and thus the actions of people in general. This importance of opinion makers is well known, of course, and I respect the truism only to insure you that I take very seriously what you say about Sathya Sai Baba.

I doubt if anyone who reads your words about Sathya Sai Baba could in justice say that your words are unreasonable. You are an experienced investigative reporter in the field of claims of spiritual power and spiritual leadership, and your findings certainly justify a skeptical kindly prove to me approach to even such a giant figure as Sathya Sai Baba, for to your own direct knowledge there are only the claims of some persons like me that Sathya Sai Baba is in fact what we say he is.

One difficulty is in equating the validity of Sathya Sai Baba with the fact or fiction of the materialization of objects although I do understand the viewpoint that false in one aspect, then suspect in all aspects. The materialization of objects is a very minor part of Baba's work in the world, and he attributes no proof of divine wisdom to these manifestations, simply saying the ability is natural to him whereas it is acquired by yogis after long practice and even then is not stable and permanent. As you well know, there are yogis in Burma and in India who have developed yogic or siddhi powers and the materialization of objects is one of these powers. I personally know three yogis who have siddhi powers and no doubt there are many other such yogis, and perhaps even some in the West. These powers are not proof of Divinity powers, but are powers within the capability of human persons. However, it is quite correct for a keen mind to require proof satisfactory to that mind that a particular person does indeed have an out-of-ordinary ability. Such proof is direct when the phenomenon is directly encountered. For instance, when I am sitting against Baba's knee and see his hand extended well beyond body and clothing and from his open palm in front of my eyes and in front of the eyes of a roomful of sharp-witted university students springs a rosary of 108 perfectly matched pearls, which he then gives to one of the people there, I know directly that I have witnessed an event in this relative world and that it would be unreasonable to demand that the event be repeated under laboratory controls.

Over the 19 years that I have known Baba, although I have not kept count, I have witnessed well over 100 materializations with myself in close proximity to Baba, and some of these have been most extraordinary. It would be of benefit to everyone within the—I suspect—quite large circle of your influence if when you are next in India you would pay a visit to Sathya Sai Baba, witness materializations, and then say what would be necessary to validate the experience for you. If you care to send a note if and when you go, I will do what I can to help secure an interview with Baba—this is not the easiest thing in the world in that usually from 20,000 to 50,000 people are there, each hoping and praying for an interview. Benefit to people living now arises from the worldwide social and educational work of Baba and from his profound spiritual wisdom. Even more direct is the deepening of one's understanding in which comes with opening one's heart and ears to Baba. In one's mind there opens a perception of the distinction between appearance and reality, and in one's heart foolishness weakens and there is happiness instead. David, if I may say to you, what if in actuality Sathya Sai Baba is even more than what his devotees claim, what if in fact there is an embodiment of Divinity that except for name and form is the indivisible Absolute Consciousness fully there, then would it not be a great pity to be alive without having cognized such a great wonder? Would it not be a great pity, David, to let such a happening remain unobserved by you, remain unknown to you because of intervening ideas and concepts? You go to India frequently, I believe. Why not add a day or so to your itinerary and visit Sathya Sai Baba at Whitefield or Prasanthi Nilayam, and then make a judgement? Stop over in Bangalore and in twenty minutes a taxi will carry you to Whitefield, or Baba is in Prasanthi Nilayam, then in three hours the taxi will have you there.

With appreciation of your work, and kindest regards to your goodself, --*Sincerely, Hislop [Dr. John S. Hislop]*

Although I did get a chance to go to India in March of 1988, my schedule did not allow me to visit with Sathya Sai Baba in South India. Dr. Hislop is right, however, in his insistence that a researcher see for himself (instead of relying on secondary accounts) whether or not a particular guru is genuine. Book knowledge is helpful, but not sufficient. Thus, it is vitally important to balance our rational skepticism with experiential interaction and observation. I must say also that Sathya Sai Baba's disciples have been very open and outgoing about supplying information about their guru and his teachings. Indeed, I have found Sai Baba devotees to be some of the nicest and friendliest people I have interviewed.

MODERN MIRACLES

Thankfully, there is a new book on Sathya Sai Baba which goes a long way in trying to determine the relative authenticity of his miracles. Erlendur Haraldsson's *Modern Miracles: An Investigative Report on Psychic Phenomena Associated with Sathya Sai Baba* is the first book of its kind. Haraldsson, who has gone to India eight times, approaches the alleged miracles of Sai Baba with a critical, but open outlook. Although the Icelandic professor of psychology fails to get Sathya Sai Baba to undergo controlled experiments, he does nevertheless get to the truth behind many reported miracles. A number of them Haraldsson debunks, including the famous "resurrection of Walter Cowan", it which turns out to be a fairly exaggerated yarn (Haraldsson interviewed the attending doctors and none of them ever reported Cowan dying; he was very sick, they reported, but that's it.) However, Haraldsson is quick to point out that there have not been any confirmed reports of Sai Baba using sleight of hand tricks to produce vibhutti or other religious artifacts. Simply put, there's no scientific proof that Sai Baba's does miracles (only suggestive accounts and testimonies) but there is also no evidence at this stage of fraud. The paradox of Sai Baba remains. I highly recommend *Modern Miracles* to all UCSM readers. Undoubtedly, Haraldsson's study is the most balanced book ever written on the miraculous work of Sathya Sai Baba. Another book that touches upon the Sathya Sai Baba controversy, at least from a skeptical perspective, is Tal Brooke's *Lord of the Air*, which has been republished in India in a paperback version titled, *Avatar of Night*. Although Brooke's work is basically a polemic, it does provide the reader with an inside glimpse (and a contrary interpretation) of the life and work of Sathya Sai Baba.

WALTER COWAN'S DEATH AND RESURRECTION
(*Excerpt from B.C. Skeptics*)

As I mentioned in the previous section, Hislop is the major proponent of this anecdote in North America. David Lane is a researcher and editor of the journal mentioned below in Hislop's letter. He is broadly sympathetic with religious aims and is concerned to separate the unreliable from the more reliable forms and claims of religion. When he read Haraldsson's book, he wrote Hislop, and Hislop gave this response.

Hislop's explanation of Cowan's death and resurrection

It was very kind of you to send me the Research Issue of your most excellent Journal (UCSM). Many thanks... Dr. Heraldsson's conclusion is that the story is false because there is no objective evidence that Cowan died, and that statements made about the incident are themselves false. On the other hand, unless I am to be considered as either lying or in error when I quoted Sathya Sai Baba, there is the other side. Since I did quote Sathya Sai Baba correctly there being several conversations between us on the topic it really boils down to the issue of whether or not Sathya Sai Baba was lying. Dr. Heraldsson's conclusion has to be taken, I believe, that because of statements made by the hospital's doctor and by Judge Damadar Rao the proper conclusion is that Cowan did not die and therefore Baba lied when he told me (and others) that Cowan had died and had been brought back to life, not once only but on three occasions. I do not see how this inference can be escaped... Two points placed into emphasis by Dr. Heraldsson were the denials of the doctor at the hospital in Madras, and the denial of Judge Damadar Rao.

Mrs. Cowan told me that the doctor came to her at her hotel and demanded that she provide him with a ticket and with sponsorship to the USA. This she would not do and according to her, the doctor's denials arose thereafter. Judge Damadar Rao is a fine Indian gentleman, respected and admired by everyone who knows him. His son is the Principal of the Sathya Sai Men's College at Whitefield. The Judge and his wife, long-time devotees of Sathya Sai Baba, are now living their retirement years in Baba's Ashram, Prasanthi Nilayam, at Puttaparthi. I do not see how Judge Damadar's statement and mine can ever be reconciled. When Dr. Heraldsson asked the Judge, some thirteen or fourteen years after the incident, the Judge's memory was as stated in Dr. Haraldsson's book. When I set forth my account, about a month after the event, my memory was that the Judge told me he had independently gone to the hospital the day following Cowan's death and verified the circumstances of his admittance to the hospital. How can I now deny my memory of that time, and how can the Judge deny his present memory? Neither is possible. Each of us is saying the truth to the best of his knowledge. Thus, I can see no end to the different stories about Walter Cowan's `resurrection'.... Thanks again for the Journal, and for our past communications. —John S. Hislop

SATHYA SAI BABA EXPLOITS: LETTER ONE

Hello Professor Lane, as we had talked, I am giving you a thorough account of my experiences with Sai Baba. I hope that this will be of interest to people and will help them to understand what Baba is all about. Thank you for giving me the chance to write this essay. I first got to know of Sai Baba in 1985 or 1986 through my brother.

I visited Sai Baba three times, on three straight summers. Once I stayed there one and half months, another time I stayed two and half months and the last time I was there for three and half. My first two trips I had seven interviews and a total of seven private interviews, with just me and Baba in the private interview room. Baba had materialized a gold ring with three stones which he told me were diamonds. The ring did not fit the finger on which Baba had placed it but I left it there regardless, as that was the finger Baba had chosen to put it on. Here I would like to mention that of the four rings which Baba has "materialized" for my family and myself, none of them fit correctly. In all the books regarding the "miracles" of Sai Baba you will read that ALL such rings fit the person perfectly. I have never read a book were it was told that almost all rings fit perfectly. And also, later I found out that the stones were not diamonds. The stones after a while got black and two of the three fell out. I took this to mean that Baba is angry at me for not being good, for not practicing his teachings as well as I COULD, for trying and not doing. Another thing that was interesting was that Baba would not be able to tell things correctly. In one instance I was told by him that the night before I had fever. I didn't, neither was I in any kind of heat. :o) Perhaps he wanted me to, but I wasn't. I just let it go, destroyed it right there and then, that very instant. No doubts were allowed.

In my first private interview, Baba did a ceremony which is supposed to be sacred in Hinduism and is done to all the followers by their gurus. This practice involves the guru putting oil on his hand and pushing his hand upward between the front testicle and the back area. That area is supposed to be a special area which is very important to spiritual practice of the devotee. This action is supposed to awaken this area, which is supposedly full of energy, which will then play an important role in the thought of the devotees. In my case, it was more of the opposite and my thoughts were never changed for the better. I was getting worse as time passed.

In every private interview after that Baba would ask me to put down my pants while he massaged my testicle. I would reason that Baba perhaps is passing some energy to that area. Perhaps I had damaged that area or something in that area by playing with myself. I had found reasons in order to destroy any doubts that might come to mind. In one occasion, Baba was not just massaging it, he was trying to give me a hard on. The thought that he is doing so came to my mind then, but of course I destroyed it. Now, as an ex-devotee, I am able to see and think about what he was doing, rather than destroy it. At this interview, as he was pushing his hand back and forth on my testicle, I was telling him about many different things on my mind. Of course, I was so sure that he is doing the best thing for me that I was thinking of something else. I was telling him about the problems in my country of Iran, how the people are suffering, the problems of my family and my own problems. He couldn't get me hard so all of a sudden with anger and an angry face he threw my thing up against my stomach and with an angry face he turned his back to me. I thought he is probably angry at me because I should have more faith in him, he already knows all my problems, everything in my mind, and he will help me in whatever way he can. Actually, he was angry that I didn't get hard and so when he turned towards me he told me to put my pants up again. This was the only occasion which he kept some distance between me and him while he was playing with me. Every other time, he would hug me and do it. My question to those who believe that Baba's intentions in playing with me was pure is that if Baba says not a blade of grass moves without his will, then why does he have to touch me in that way to perform whatever pure intention or will he had in mind? Or is it that when he was playing with me, he was being good to me by giving me the privilege of being close to him and interact with him? For those who are not following, Sai followers believe that Baba knows all our inner thoughts and the reason why he talks to us is because he is trying to talk to us for our own enjoyment. He really doesn't have to talk at all or ask us questions regarding our lives since he is the All-knowing. He does so for our sake, so that we can talk to him and interact with him. Could it be that Sai Baba was playing with me in order to satisfy my needs to interact with him? And what kind of satisfaction did he - or do you - think I would get from that kind of interaction?

In almost all of such interviews, Baba would breath harder and sometimes he would make noises too. Something I forgot to tell you about the private interview above was that while I was telling Baba about these problems, his face was getting uneasy while he constantly, the whole time was looking down at my testicle. His eyebrows got twisted and his face got more and more upset as he was trying to play with me. I wonder why? He sometimes would tell me that I was weak there, there was too much being wasted from there, etc. Why then did he touch it? Was he fixing things? Why did he have to fix things by touching and rubbing and going back and forth?

In one interview, he stood up while I was kneeling on my knees. With his right hand, took my head and put it against his stomach. With his left hand he took my right hand and put it against his testicle. He rubbed my hand there for a short while and this time he was making loud noises of .... I tried to look up to his face to see it, but he pushed my head hard against his stomach and did not allow me to look up. So, I didn't try again. While he took my hand there, I felt his testicle, although I didn't grab it, I just let him direct my hand and do whatever he wants. At the same time, I would touch him by the outside part of my hand. As I said before, he was making loud voices while he was doing that. This took about two minutes before he let go of me and my hand and said "This is God"!!! Whatever!!! It was his way of putting a controlled mind to think and find many answers to what that whole situation was all about. It was his way of covering the sick idea of having me touch him, and also covering his loud, wild voices. Anyhow, those of you who have a clear and logical mind understand me.

I had these experiences and still it took me over six months to deal with the movie that I mentioned before. After dealing with this movie, I went to look over some of the movies which we had about Baba. These movies are movies which are prevalent within Sai devotees. The very first movie which I watched is called "God lives in India". In that movie they showed about four or five instances which Baba cheats the "materialization" of ash - ash is supposedly holy and is supposedly being created by Baba from thin air. One of these instances is a very close, clear shot which shows Baba take something with his right hand from underneath of some letters in his left hand while bending over a bit to talk to someone. He then takes the letters by his right hand and cleans his left hand. Then he takes the letters from the right hand and immediately starts to motion his right hand in circular motion which is a "sign" that he is going to create something out of thin air. This shot is a close-up and very clear. After seeing this first movie, I knew the truth and didn't watch any other movies. I am sure if the other movies have segments that show Baba's actions twenty seconds prior to each "creation" of ash or whatever, you can see him cheating.

More recently, there was a movie on cable TV here in the US which showed Baba cheat on materialization of a ring or necklace, I don't remember. There was much argument about it on the internet newsgroups. Bon Govani, a Sai devotee, defended his opinion of what the movie showed by saying each person saw a different thing. What everyone, including Bon agree on is that Baba does some weird thing with his hand under a plate before he brings down his hand and starts to circle his hand. Sai devotees have their own way of thinking and so their own reasons and answers. It will be impossible to convince these people on anything. The more you use your reasons to find something or some way to prove your points, the more they will use their twisted reasoning to counter attack your ideas. Their counter attack is 99% illogical since they are used to twisting things around. Besides what good is a logical path which starts with "Baba is God..."? Baba is God, therefore, he couldn't have cheated on that movie, therefore, everyone sees a different thing when they see that movie. They don't think that what kind of motion is Baba making? Why is he making that motion? Why is he making it under the plate? Why the need of that motion? Etc.

So, I am looking forward to getting a lot of illogical responses to this essay. I welcome them and look forward to disproving any illogical ideas. I hope that their responses and my replies will give all of you a hint of how brainwashed the Sai devotees are and what a sorry state of mind they have. Hopefully, those Sai devotees who still have some reason left can benefit substantially from this and can overcome all mind control tricks that have been imposed on them. And, hopefully, all those who are considering Sai Baba, would have the luck to see these postings and can benefit from them too. I really hope so.

One thing that I forgot to say is that on my last trip to India, there were about 20 American and Indian American college students which came to attend Baba's summer classes which mainly concentrate on spirituality. Some of these students considered themselves devotees, others had come to see and judge Baba for themselves. In an interview Baba "materialized" a ring or something else for either all of those students or majority of them. At least half of those students say that they saw Baba CHEAT. They reported that they saw Baba take and put things from the sides or back - I don't remember which one they said - of the chair that he was seating on. When I say the sides or the back I mean the sides of the cushion of the chair or the backside of the cushion. These students were firm in what they saw. After this interview, some four days later, Baba was out giving darshan - walking around, sometimes stopping to talk to some individuals, sometimes choosing individuals or groups of individuals for an interview. He stopped in front of the American students which were sitting in an area that was designated to them. He made the circular motion, and supposedly created some ash and threw it on one of the student's face. During this time, his back was to me. When he turned around I saw his face was very angry. He was pissed! As usual, as you know why, I didn't give importance to this. Later, one of the boys in the American group, with whom I had become very close told me that this student who was thrown ash to face and eyes was very vocal about what they had seen in the interview room, namely, Baba taking things from the chair on which he sat on. Now, if Baba's life is his message as he says so, then is it right that we act in this way when someone criticizes us? I am sure I'll get a few reasons as to why Baba did such a thing. Or at best, I might get something like Baba's intentions are not known to us and that I can't say why he did that. I'll be looking forward to reading the reasons.

SATHYA SAI BABA EXPLOITS: LETTER TWO

Dear Dave,
I was a Sai Devotee for about 4 years. In that time I had several interviews with Sai Baba. On my final trip to Sai Baba, I began to question his philosophy and powers. On that trip, among other things, I examined closely the process which he "materialized" objects. It soon became clear to me that he used sleight of hand. He hides rings between cushions, etc. It is not hard to recognize, if you want to see the truth in the situation. I soon left the organization. I am interested in finding more people like myself. Unfortunately I had experiences similar to those described by Tal Brooke. I have unsuccessfully tried to contact him. Do you have any advice for me? Regards, [name redacted]

SATHYA SAI BABA EXPLOITS: LETTER THREE

Dear Dave,
My first witness account of sleight of hand was in Brindaven. I saw Baba come out of the personal interview room and sit down. As he was sitting there I noticed a large gold watch under his small hand, which he was unsuccessfully trying to hide. A moment later he made the familiar circular motion with his hand as if he were materializing the object, and then gave a student the watch. On another occasion I saw Sai Baba reach between the cushions of his chair for something, and then moments later he made the circular motion and showed everyone a small container filled with vibhuti, the gray ash. I then noticed that behind the cushion in his chair there was something shiny, and he paid careful attention to correct the position of the cushion to

hide the object. Another time I saw him take a worn bracelet from a man, then with his hand cupped blew on it three times at the same time moving his hand up and down. On the final movement, he tossed the chain into the side of his chair so it slid down between the inside of the chairs large arm and his leg. He then discreetly took took something from his other hand and made the circular motion and gave the man a new bracelet. What is really funny about that situation is that Sai Baba forgot to take the old bracelet from his chair when he left, so when he got up, there it lay in plain view for everyone in the room. A student I was with, and who was very devoted to Baba, picked it up and looked at it, confirming that it was the old bracelet. When Baba returned and noticed his mistake, he scolded this student, who was sitting right at the foot of Baba's chair and could not miss the bracelet. Then Baba sat and in a flash picked up the bracelet and very discreetly tossed it into the outside upper corner of the arm of the chair. There were no visible pockets there, but there is a very large seam, and the arms of the chair are huge enough to store lots of things. The student, in the first account, who received the watch is an American who emigrated from India. He came from a very wealthy family in India who were big contributors to the Sai cause. What I came to realize, is there is a system in India similiar to our mafia. Very prominent families in India support gurus who have great political power, and this is how these families have their influence over political policy. Of course I don't have any evidence for all this, but in my conversations with students at Sai's University, this was explained to me. It is also well known that prominent figures in the Indian government make fairly frequent stops to visit with Sai Baba, including the president of India. (I was in India when the president came to visit Sai Baba. When this happens there is huge comotion and Indians crowd darshan to see the president, not Sai Baba). The students also know that Sai is a hoax, that he does not materialise a thing. However they are getting a very inexpensive education, so they keep their mouths shut. The student I talked with most, would not tell me other things that he knew, but I am sure that it had to do with the students who spent the night with Baba. I know this because this is where he would no longer answer my questions. Everyone knows that Sai Baba has students spend the night with him. They stay up to "serve" him at night. It's a very well-kept secret as to how they serve Sai Baba, but little will come out because no student wants to be kicked out of Sai Baba's school.

As stated, they are receiving a very good educations there, very inexpensively. I say very inexpensively because many believe it to be free, but this is not the case. Students pay for room and board, which to many is rather expensive. The education part is free, but there are bills.

This brings me to my very questionable experiences with Sai Baba. On my second trip to Sai Baba I had four interviews. Each time I saw Baba, his hand would gradually make more prominent connections to my groin. The first interview was a slight swipe, the second a definite touch and the third time he grabbed me and with a very stern face looked me directly in the eye and said "you are very weak!" Needless to say, he scared and embarrassed me. I was guilt ridden to have sexual passion, though I was a healthy 16 year old boy, a testosterone machine. I was not going to talk to anyone about the experience. In the final interview he asked me to take my pants down. I was totally confused, so he took them down for me. He then made vibhutti and rubbed it on my genitals. On my third trip, he did the same thing, but rubbed oil on my genitals. Fortunately I was never taken advantage of any worse, but I was humiliated when I realised his true intentions, and I felt I had really lost an innocence that I would have cherished keeping.

When I finally did talk about what happened to me, the first two reactions were to never speak of it with others because the whole thing would be taken out of context and misconstrued. Then I talked to others my own age and they told me of similar experiences. I even heard terrible stories of children who would meet with Sai Baba twice a week to play "sex games" and the like. Oral sex and masturbation were common in these meetings. Many of my own friends told me about attempts by Sai Baba to touch them, but they wouldn't let him.

THE DEATH OF SAI BABA NEWS REPORT
Bloomberg Newswire

Cricketers Sachin Tendulkar and Sunil Gavaskar joined tens of thousands of devotees to pay homage to Sathya Sai Baba, the Indian spiritual guru whose charities and claimed miracles won him both devotion and scorn.

"He is going to live in our hearts permanently," former Indian cricket captain Gavaskar told reporters in the southern town of Puttaparthi in Andhra Pradesh state where Sai Baba, who died yesterday aged 84, built his ashram. "He will still

71

continue to inspire us," Gavaskar said in a televised address. Politicians and film stars were also among followers who queued for a last glimpse of the preacher, taking turns to kneel besides his saffron-robed body placed in a glass casket at the town's Sai Kulwant Hall. A state funeral is scheduled for Tuesday.

"At least 200,000 devotees have paid their respects. Schools and other establishments are closed," senior police official B. Narasimhalu said in a phone interview. Hard Rock Café founder Isaac Tigrett sold his stake in the restaurant chain and donated the entire proceeds of $108 million to Sai Baba for a specialty hospital in Puttaparthi to provide free health care to the rural poor, the Open magazine reported in April. Sai Baba, who sported afro-style hair reminiscent of rock musician Jimi Hendrix, died after his heart and respiratory organs failed, A.N. Safaya, director at the Sri Sathya Sai Baba Institute of Higher Medical Sciences, said in a statement on the hospital's website. Sai Baba "endeared himself to the people through various institutions," Prime MinisterManmohan Singh said in a statement yesterday. "He believed that it is the duty of every person to ensure that all people have access to the basic requirements for sustenance of life."

Sai Baba's trust has set up schools, universities and hospitals, with various Indian political leaders providing support for his charities. Former Prime Minister P.V. Narasimha Rao and ex-president Shankar Dayal Sharma were present during the opening of a water project in 1995 in Andhra Pradesh state, while former premier Atal Bihari Vajpayee inaugurated a hospital in Bangalore.

At the age of 14, the guru told his family that he would be known as "Sai Baba," the title of a past Indian ascetic of whom he claimed to be a reincarnation, according to a statement on his website. In 1960, he told his followers he would "leave his body" in 2019.

While devotees believe in his miracles, including acts of producing holy ash, rings and necklaces, fruits, sugar candy and watches out of thin air, critics have dismissed them as tricks.

They "remained controversial to others and he shied away from scientific tests that would have settled forever the issue of their genuineness," said Erlendur Haraldsso, professor emeritus, faculty of social sciences at the University of Iceland, who did research on Indian "miracle-makers." Allegations by some former devotees that Sathya Sai Baba had sexually abused them tarnished his image. K. Chakravarty, secretary of the Sri Sathya Sai Central Trust didn't answer calls made to his office yesterday.

"We don't regard him as a genuine miracle worker," said David C. Lane, a professor of sociology and philosophy at San Antonio College in Texas. "I have a number of reports from former disciples that they were molested under the guise of spiritual unfoldment." Sai Baba denied all charges against him and has not been charged with any offenses in India.

WHEN PROPHECY FAILS
News report: The Times of India

HYDERABAD: Though the condition of spiritual leader Sathya Sai Baba is worsening, some of his devotees are confident he will recover and live for 96 years as he had once predicted. A group of eminent devotees, including former judges, police officers and physicians, believe that the 85-year-old Sathya Sai Baba's present condition is because he has taken on himself the sufferings of one of his devotees. As the guru battles for life at the Sathya Sai super speciality hospital at Puttaparthi town in Anantapur district, a group of devotees on Thursday held a press conference here to say he would recover and appeal to the media to respect their sentiments.

POSTSCRIPT

Sathya Sai Baba died at the age of 84 on April 24th, 2011

7 | The Material Basis of NDEs

Early in the morning of January 30, 2014, I became aware of a recent interview of Patricia Smith Churchland, the renowned neurophilosopher, which was conducted via telephone by Alex Tsakiris which was posted on his website *Skeptiko.com* under the tabloid like headline: ***"Dr. Patricia Churchland sandbagged by near-death experience questions."***

Since I have been aware of Professor Churchland's ideas since the early 1980s when she first arrived at UCSD (along with her equally respected philosopher-husband Paul) where I was also teaching and doing work on my Ph.D., I was intrigued to find out precisely how she got "sandbagged."

Interestingly, that very morning I also noticed that the interview had gone somewhat viral, as I received several letters and postings from various parts of the globe directing me to the interview and lambasting Churchland for her responses to Tsakiris.

However, after reading the transcript and listening to the taped recording of the interview, I initially thought it was much ado about a simple misunderstanding over sentence construction and its contextual intention. But the more I read varying commentaries on the interview both on *Skeptiko* itself and elsewhere (particularly on the Yahoo forum *Radhasoami Studies*), I realized that Churchland's materialistic view that consciousness is a product of the brain was touching a very sensitive nerve (to coopt the very title of Patricia's latest book) amongst those who hold that consciousness cannot be materially reduced to the substratum of our central nervous system.

Perhaps what is most interesting in the current Churchland controversy is not necessarily her physicalist perspective or her contestable citation of Dr. Pim van Lommel, but the vitriolic reaction to how she conducted herself during the interview and her promoting of eliminative materialism.

Tsakiris simply doesn't like Churchland answers and thus appears more interested in creating a faux debate based on his own resistance to neurophilosophy and what it portends.

I think it might be instructive to take a closer examination of Alex Tsakiris' interview and perhaps look a bit deeper at why there has been such an outcry against a purely materialist understanding of consciousness and near-death experiences.

Patricia Churchland has long argued that the best way to go about understanding consciousness is to focus on how the brain itself works. In this regard, she is perhaps best known for her pioneering introductory textbook, Neurophilosophy. In the journal *Progress in Brain Research*, Churchland details her approach,

Explaining the nature and mechanisms of conscious experience in neurobiological terms seems to be an attainable, if yet unattained, goal. Research at many levels is important, including research at the cellular level that explores the role of recurrent pathways between thalamic nuclei and the cortex, and research that explores consciousness from the perspective of action. Conceptually, a clearer understanding of the logic of expressions such as 'causes' and 'correlates', and about what to expect from a theory of consciousness are required.

In Churchland's latest book, *Touching a Nerve: The Self as Brain* she devotes chapter three, "My Heavens", to exploring the physiological basis behind near-death experiences. She doesn't doubt that some individuals who are pronounced clinically dead report having wonderful luminous experiences (seeing inner light or entering tunnels or feeling bliss, etc), what she doubts is whether such experiences are "beyond" the brain's own capacity to produce such illuminations. As Churchland cautions,

Here is what I want to know: Were all the people who reported a near-death experience actually dead or merely near death? One thing to keep in mind is that even once the heart has stopped, there may be residual brain activity for a short period—longer if oxygen is supplied. Were the subjects actually brain dead? Brain death is taken to imply that the critical brain regions for sustaining heartbeat and breathing (regions in the brainstem) no longer function, and the patient shows no brainstem reflexes, such as the pupil contracting when a light is shone on the eye. Some 25 different assessments are used to determine brain death. If, for example, there is some residual brainstem and cortical activity, then the brain is not dead. Then odd experiences may result.

Churchland clearly doubts that those reporting near-death experiences (keeping in mind that only a minority of such patients—anywhere from 12 to 18 percent in one major study—ever recall having one) were, in fact, completely brain dead, since more sophisticated brain imaging techniques indicate that subtle neural activity may be still be operative. As Churchland radically asserts,

"One fairly reliable way to assess the prospects of a patient in coma after severe anoxia, such as in drowning, is to image the brain twice, separated by several days. If the brain is severely damaged, substantial shrinkage will be observed in the images over the course of a few days. Shrinkage is seen more frequently in severe oxygen deprivation (anoxia) than in head trauma. When shrinkage is seen, the prospects for recovery of function are vanishingly small. In children, determining brain death requires two assessments separated by a time delay of several days, with the second assessment performed by a different physician than the one who performed the first assessment. To the best of my knowledge, not a single patient who has been credibly diagnosed as brain dead according to the aforementioned criteria has come to consciousness and reported seeing dead relatives, divine persons, or angels while brain dead. This suggests a more modest interpretation of experiences of life after death: patients who report 'coming back from the dead' were not in fact brain dead, though they must have suffered other effects that prevented them from emerging into full consciousness, such as lowered levels of oxygen and some swelling of the brain."

To Churchland's credit, her overarching claim (that certain "brain dead" states will not yield NDE's) is a scientifically testable one and open to falsification. In this regard, she has rightly made herself vulnerable to being wrong. That is all to her credit, since it may backfire and end up lending more support those who argue that NDE's really are glimpses of something beyond the mind-body complex.

Carl Sagan, perhaps with less elegance, also posited a testable hypothesis concerning why NDE's were part and parcel of the brain when he argued in his 1979 book, *Broca's Brain: Reflections on the Romance of Science*. In a master stroke of reductionism Sagan posited that NDE's were not glimpses of heaven but rather vague birth memories of one's obstetrician or mid-wife.

As Sagan poetically put it, "[At the] end of the birth process, when the child's head has penetrated the cervix and might, even if the eyes are closed, perceive a tunnel illuminated at one end and sense the brilliant radiance of the extrauterine world. The discovery of light for a creature that has lived its entire existence in darkness must be a profound and on some level an unforgettable experience. And there, dimly made out by the low resolution of the newborn's eyes, is some godlike figure surrounded by a halo of light—the Midwife or the Obstetrician or the Father. At the end of a monstrous travail, the baby flies away from the uterine universe, and rises toward the lights and the gods."

Sagan's theory that NDE's were in actuality BBM's (being born memories) recalled because of severe birth trauma was widely publicized when it came out and even made for a popular article in *Reader's Digest* entitled "The Amniotic Universe." While some theorists championed Sagan's ideas at first, on closer inspection it turned out to be wildly overstated and didn't withstand closer scrutiny.

As Susan Blackmore concluded as early as 1983, "Since the theory has failed this first simple test I think we can say that the comparison of the OBE with birth experiences is a superficially appealing analogy but, in terms of prediction, an unhelpful one."

Churchland, like Sagan before her, is deeply skeptical that NDE's are indicative of something trans-neuronal, since the brain has an amazing plasticity to virtually simulate almost anything imaginable, particularly when deprived of external checks and balances which may cast doubt on its almost intrinsic hallucinatory nature. In this regard, Churchland thinks it is important to draw parallels to drug induced revelries since there are many commonalities with NDE's. As Churchland points out,

"Out-of-body and other dissociative episodes can be induced by ketamine, the drug sometimes used in anesthesia. According to my students, ketamine has now become a party drug, allowing them to explore the sensation of floating above their body, having their mind vacate their body, and so forth. That such purely physical interventions can induce experiences qualitatively similar to those called near-death experiences speaks strongly in favor of a neurobiological basis, one that can eventually be discovered through research."

It right here, however, where Churchland's analysis of Dr. Pim van Lommel's 2001 study (co-authored with Ruud van Wees, Vincent Meyers, and Ingrid Elfferich), "Near-Death Experience in Survivors of Cardiac Arrest: A Prospective Study in the Netherlands," in the prestigious journal, *Lancet*, has generated a recent onslaught of criticism. Although Churchland provides the substance of Van Lommel's groundbreaking findings, how she has chosen to describe his results has drawn severe criticism from a cadre of Internet critics.

On pages 70 and 71 of the print version of *Touching a Nerve*, Churchland summarizes the most dramatic features of Van Lommel's report in this fashion, "In one large study of 344 patients who suffered cardiac arrest, only about 12 percent (62) reported a core near-death experience (tunnel with light, felt dead, felt peacefulness). Others may have had an experience but no memory of it, because, of course, the study relied on post-resuscitation reports. Only 50 percent of the 62 patients who did have near-death experiences had the feeling that they were dead; only 56 percent (35) of the 62 patients had positive feeling such as peacefulness; only 24 percent (15) had the experience of leaving the body; only 31 percent (19) had the experience of moving through a tunnel; only 23 percent (14) had an experience with light."

Churchland then ponders, not merely rhetorically, the following, "If heaven really awaits us all after death, it is a little puzzling that only 12 percent of resuscitated patients reported a near-death experience with tunnels and light and peacefulness." Churchland, ever looking for a physical basis behind NDE's, follows up with her most revealing question, "Is it plausible that there will be a neurobiological explanation of the cluster of phenomena?"

Certainly this is a vital question to ask, particularly given Churchland's empirical modus operandi, but instead of merely focusing on her own affirmative answer in this respect, she attempts to buttress her reasoning by citing Dr. Pim van Lommel himself, writing

As neuroscientist Pim van Lommel and his colleagues pointed out, a strong reason for saying yes is that experiences similar to those suffering anoxia following cardiac arrest can be induced by electrical stimulation of the temporal lobe and hippocampus, something that may be done in epileptic patients prior to surgery. Similar experiences can also be induced by raising the level of carbon dioxide (hypercapnia, sometimes suffered by scuba divers) or by decreasing oxygen levels in the brain by hyperventilating following the Valsalva maneuver (as when you strain at stool).

In referencing Dr. Van Lommel in this specific way, Alex Tsakiris felt that Churchland was inappropriately lending credence to her materialist agenda since Van Lommel doesn't share Churchland's brain as self thesis. Tsakiris believed that Churchland was spinning Van Lommel in a direction he never himself intended.

_____

Alex Tsakiris: Well, I guess one of the things I did want to ask you is in your book you ask the question, "Is there a neurobiological explanation for near-death experience?" Then you cite NDE researcher and a former guest on this show as answering that question with yes. You say that Dr. Pim van Lommel believes the answer is yes. Is that your understanding of his research?

Dr. Patricia Churchland: Well, I think there's certainly quite a bit of evidence that at least some near-death experiences have a neurobiological basis. Of course, we can't be sure about all of them. Maybe you had one that doesn't have a neurobiological basis. I wouldn't really know, would I?

Alex Tsakiris: Well specifically, Dr. Churchland, you cite in your book that Dr. Pim van Lommel holds that opinion. That's clearly not the case. I mean, he's written...

Dr. Patricia Churchland: Has he? Uh-huh (Yes).

Alex Tsakiris: Right. Do you want me to read to you what he's written? He's written that "The study of patients with near-death experience (and this is from The Lancet paper that you're citing) clearly shows us that..."

———————

What fueled the ire of a large number of commentators to the Churchland interview (besides how she comported herself) was the belief that she had misleadingly cited Van Lommel in order to prop up her own NDE as purely brain induced hypothesis. A close study of Van Lommel's *Lancet* paper does indicate, however, that he too feels that there are certain components of NDE's that must have a neurobiological basis since he writes, "And yet, neurophysiological processes must play some part in NDE. Similar experiences can be induced through electrical stimulation of the temporal lobe (and hence of the hippocampus) during neurosurgery for epilepsy, with high carbon dioxide levels (hypercarbia), and in decreased cerebral perfusion resulting in local cerebral hypoxia as in rapid acceleration during training of fighter pilots, or as in hyperventilation followed by valsalva manoeuvre. Ketamine-induced experiences resulting from blockage of the NMDA receptor, and the role of endorphin, serotonin, and enkephalin have also been mentioned, as have near-death-like experiences after the use of LSD, psilocarpine, and mescaline. These induced experiences can consist of unconsciousness, out-of-body experiences, and perception of light or flashes of recollection from the past."

But, in a revealing transition, Van Lommel makes a sharp distinction between drug-induced ecstasies (which include OBE's and phosphenic visions) and NDE's because of the latter's transformative qualities.

As Van Lommel argues, "These recollections, however, consist of fragmented and random memories unlike the panoramic life-review that can occur in NDE. Further, transformational processes with changing life-insight and disappearance of fear of death are rarely reported after induced experiences. Thus, induced experiences are not identical to NDE, and so, besides age, an unknown mechanism causes NDE by stimulation of neurophysiological and neurohumoral processes at a subcellular level in the brain in only a few cases during a critical situation such as clinical death. These processes might also determine whether the experience reaches consciousness and can be recollected."

Churchland seems quite aware of Van Lommel's distinction (which contravenes her own more sweeping connection with drug inducements) because right after citing Van Lommel's *Lancet* study, she proceeds to give her own theory about why NDE's are so transformative.

"To be sure, in contrast to hyperventilating following Valsalva, nearly dying may be transformative, for then the end of life cannot be very far away, and the reality of death is starkly evident. In such circumstances, people will be inclined to reevaluate their lives, relive memories, and reexamine what matters in life. They do this regardless of whether they believe in heaven or not. That very reexamination may be the transformative element in those who do have an unusual experience. The experience merely triggers the reflection that is transformative."

Perhaps one of the reasons Churchland has received so much flack from those advocating a spiritual interpretation of NDE's is that she consistently tries to upend transcendental explanations with more grounded ones and in the process may give the impression of being somewhat flippant in her consideration of alternative hypotheses. Calling NDE's "brain oddities" and such is reminiscent of Carl Sagan's ad hoc reductionism of out-body experiences as "a miswiring in human neuranatomy."

Such language choices can be seen as dismissive and disrespectful to those who feel strongly that what they and others have experienced deserves more than cursory rebuttals that don't fully address the complexity of what they perceive as glimpses of a wholly numinous realm.

Churchland, of course, will readily concede that she cannot prove that heaven doesn't exist or that NDE's couldn't potentially offer previews of an afterlife, but the thrust of her argument is unmistakable in its import when she writes, "This list of perceptual oddities reminds us that the brain may do surprising things, things that have no special significance regarding afterlife or past life or spiritual life. They are just neuro-oddities for which we do not—not yet, anyhow—have complete explanations. Fascinating, poorly explained, sometimes annoying or disturbing, they are what they are: oddities."

Van Lommel appears more open to a less materialist explanation of NDE's, though he appreciates its brain related underpinnings. Comments Van Lommel, "How could a clear consciousness outside one's body be experienced at the moment that the brain no longer functions during a period of clinical death with flat EEG? Also, in cardiac arrest the EEG usually becomes flat in most cases within about 10s from onset of syncope. Furthermore, blind people have described veridical perception during out-of-body experiences at the time of this experience. NDE pushes at the limits of medical ideas about the range of human consciousness and the mind-brain relation."

In reviewing Churchland's citation of Van Lommel, it is debatable whether she intended to hijack him into her camp by only focusing on where they agreed (looking for certain neurobiological correlations) or was rather merely underlining his own conclusion in the *Lancet* where he encouraged more, not less, empirical work when he wrote,

Research should be concentrated on the effort to explain scientifically the occurrence and content of NDE. Research should be focused on certain specific elements of NDE, such as out-of-body experiences and other verifiable aspects.

Interestingly, how we parse Churchland's one sentence reference to Van Lommel and how we contextualize it within *Touching a Nerve's* chapter on NDE's may be more reflective of our own particular interests and emphases than with any objective indices about Churchland's ulterior motives or lack thereof.

What is even more intriguing, at least in terms of human psychology, is to witness how Alex Tsakiris and others who sided with his particular twist reacted to Patricia Churchland's demeanor during the telephone interview that apparently suffered a series of technical mishaps.

Here is how Alex Tsakiris characterized Churchland's responses: "It was stunning to me. It was laughable. In fact, I think you heard he [sic: me? her?] laugh a couple of times. Here's a woman... I can hear the background noise and yet she's suggesting that there's some kind of malfunction in the equipment and that's the reason why she can't respond to my questions. I just offer up one question and it's a recurring question on Skeptiko and that is: What's going on here? How have we devolved into a scientific and academic system that props up such nonsense? Again, the really scary thing about Dr. Churchland is that her opinion is the status quo majority opinion. It's nonsensical; it's indefensible, but it's the majority opinion. And don't question it."

A number of respondents to Tsakiris' interview felt that Churchland consciously hung up on him because she was backed into a corner about misappropriating Van Lommel's opinion and was afraid of taking any more heat. Jason Enger's own comment is indicative of several others:

"Her dubious claims about technical difficulties don't explain her bad arguments, bad responses, hesitations, and silence during the times when she was responding to you and wasn't claiming any technical difficulties. And when she did claim to be experiencing technical problems, she didn't come across as convincing. She's a poor actress. And why would she let her interaction with you end in that manner, if there was nothing other than technical issues involved in ending the telephone interview? Why didn't she email you an explanation of what she said about Pim van Lommel, for example? Why would she let the interview end that way if she was being honest? I'd expect an honest person to quickly email you with the relevant information. Maybe she'll email you with some sort of response in the future or provide a response to somebody else if asked for one or pressured to give one. But the fact that she didn't quickly provide you with a response, whether over the telephone or otherwise, is revealing."

Having witnessed how Patricia Churchland has responded in the past to sharp, critical questions (via telephony to boot), I personally don't buy that she was afraid of Tsakiris' criticism as much as she may have been put off by his tone. For example, back in the spring of 1990 one of my brightest students at the time, Meredith Doran (who is now a Professor of French Literature at Penn State), conducted an in-depth telephone interview of Patricia Churchland on behalf of our newly formed philosophy journal, *Plato's Cave*. At that time Meredith Doran had a distinctively spiritual viewpoint and didn't share Churchland's eliminative materialist perspective. However, Churchland was quite engaging and open to critical feedback throughout the interview process and even went the extra mile to explain her views in a clear and forthright manner. A large part of this interview was originally published as a small booklet entitled, *A Glorious Piece of Meat, the Dalai Lama, and the Neural Basis of Consciousness*. It has had a wide circulation and recently was published on *Integral World* under the abbreviated title "The Neural Basis of Consciousness".

Alex Tsakris later criticized Churchland for apparently not being prepared for the interview and dodging his hard questions, but Churchland immediately corrects his mistaken impression of her own views (he conflates her nuanced understanding of consciousness with his own caricatures of Daniel Dennett and Richard Dawkins) on the nature of consciousness and what it means, making one pause about who was the real unprepared participant.

Alex Tsakiris: Yeah, great. That's really an interesting place to start, this idea that consciousness is an illusion of a biological robot.

Dr. Patricia Churchland: Oh, I wouldn't say it's an illusion. It's not an illusion at all.

Alex Tsakiris: Well, this is the quote. That's what Daniel Dennett said, right?

Dr. Patricia Churchland: Yeah, but that's not what I said.

Alex Tsakiris: Okay, so it's not an illusion. What is it? Are we biological robots like Richard Dawkins thinks?

Dr. Patricia Churchland: I don't think Richard thinks that we're biological robots. I think what does seem to be emerging from science is that consciousness, for example, is a property of the physical brain. That's one of the many things actually that the physical brain does and it changes when we fall asleep. It changes when we drink alcohol. It changes when we're tired or very hungry. And it changes also as a result of changes in hormones. So if you think about your own puberty, for example, you will remember that as the levels of sex hormones and your pituitary changed and consequently as the levels of sex hormones in your brain changed, you began to think about things in a rather different way. You began to notice certain kinds of things, to pay attention, to be fixated by a certain kind of thing, and so forth. We think that consciousness is a function of the physical brain. It's a very fascinating function. It's almost certainly not unique to humans but it is a very real property of the physical brain in just the way that eye movements or many other functions like memory, attention, problem-solving, reasoning, self-control, these are all things that are properties of the physical brain.

But Tsakaris doesn't appreciate Churchland's rejoinder and resorts to calling it "splitting hairs" and responds with a series of rather confused follow-up of questions to which Churchland is forced once again to correct his mischaracterization of her philosophical views.

Alex Tsakiris: Yeah, but aren't we trying to split hairs and move away from the consciousness is an illusion thing without really jumping all the way to the other side where the physicists are taking us? They're saying that consciousness is somehow fundamental. I mean, if we break down this debate on what is the nature of consciousness, we have these two camps that we've been talking about... or I guess talking around. One is this very materialistic view like I think you started out but then I don't know if you really were holding to that... that consciousness is purely a result of an epiphenomena of the brain?

Dr. Patricia Churchland: No, it's not an epiphenomenon. It is an actual phenomenon in the physical brain. It's one of the things that the physical brain does in just the way that your brain stores memories. Some of those memories change over time as a result of changes in the physical brain. We know, for example, that people who have Alzheimer's, because they have lost many neurons in their brains, no longer have the capacity to remember certain things. Memory is a real function of the physical brain and so is consciousness. It's not an illusion; it's the real deal.

Alex Tsakiris: But what is it? I mean, I think we're dancing around. You're saying it's immaterial or it is material or it's immaterial. Don't we need to nail it down a little bit more than that? You're saying it's an emergent property of the brain. Isn't that kind of passing the buck a little bit? Here's the other possible explanation. Consciousness is somehow fundamental and the brain is somehow interacting with this consciousness which is a reality. Somehow in the field of consciousness it's out there and brain is somehow interacting with it. But that's not to confuse it with being purely a result of brain activity. I mean, that is a completely different theory, right?

Dr. Patricia Churchland: It's a theory for which there is essentially no evidence. One of the problems with that approach is that we can't understand why taking a drug, for example, should change your consciousness if consciousness is not part of the physical brain because we know that the drug changes the physical brain and that consciousness is somehow completely independent of that because it's a fundamental feature of the universe.

Alex Tsakiris: It doesn't have to be completely independent. Obviously there's some relationship, a close relationship...

Dr. Patricia Churchland: Ahh, okay. What always puzzled Descartes is if there is an independent non-physical soul, how does it interact with the physical brain? The problem with dualism is that nobody has ever been able to address that in a meaningful, testable way.

What is ironic in closely reading through this interview transcript is how clear and lucid Churchland is in her responses (whether we agree with her view or not) and how muddled Tsakiris can be in his rebuttals, particularly when he accuses her of dancing around issues.

Churchland never deviates from her materialist purview, but Tsakiris confusingly claims, "I think we're dancing around.

86

You're saying it's immaterial or it is material or it's immaterial. Don't we need to nail it down a little bit more than that?"

Yet Churchland never once indicates that consciousness was immaterial at all. Rather, she very clearly points to the neural basis of self-awareness when she says, "We know, for example, that people who have Alzheimer's, because they have lost many neurons in their brains, no longer have the capacity to remember certain things. Memory is a real function of the physical brain and so is consciousness. It's not an illusion; it's the real deal."

Tsakiris simply doesn't like Churchland answers and thus appears more interested in creating a faux debate based on his own resistance to neurophilosophy and what it portends. This becomes even more evidential when we read Tsakiris' own prefatory commentary after the interview was finished which contains a number derisive (and unnecessary?) asides that I have highlighted by italics: "She is a well-respected academic, Oxford educated, also UCSD which is a prestigious university out here in California, highly regarded at conferences, gives speeches, and has *blabbed* about these ridiculous ideas about consciousness that she has. She's *blabbed* about it for years. How else would one confront her on the nonsense that she talks about? I mean, how do you that in a nice way? How do you do that in a non-confrontational way? I don't know that you can. So it really surprised me, the extent to which she breaks down and squirms and just goes out in the outer limits of reality and believability in this interview. But I don't really know how to approach these things any other way if you really want to get answers."

Yet, in going over Churchland's answers both on audio and in the transcript I don't find her squirming in the least. She is remarkably straightforward in her views. While it is perfectly understandable that Tsakiris may not like Churchland's philosophy, what seems peculiarly odd is that he thinks she was unprepared when, in point of fact, she consistently and without equivocation presented her self as brain thesis.

Tsakiris' analysis seems primed to create a greater controversy out of the interview than it merits. The very title he uses to advertise it reads like a headline from a tabloid and has been used by Tsakiris before in his interview with Dr. Gary Marcus with the same exact heading (with only the names being changed).

Jerry Coyne, an eminent Professor in the Department of Ecology and Evolution at the University of Chicago, was also interviewed by Alex Tsakiris and had this to say about the process: "Well, this is certainly the most contentious interview I've ever had, and it's with Alex Tsakiris at Skeptiko. The 'discussion' is 57 minutes long, and things get pretty heated (it's both recorded and transcribed; I'd recommend listening to get the full flavor). When I first agreed to the interview, I was told we'd talk mainly about my book and about evolutionary biology. Several readers acquainted with the show warned me that Alex was a woo-meister who was into things like parapsychology and near-death experiences. Forewarned, I emailed Alex and he verified that we would indeed talk about evolution with perhaps a bit of discussion on the side about free will. He told me I wasn't going to be "sandbagged." LOL! It quickly became clear in the interview, though, that he wasn't much interested in evolution. . . ."

Jerry Coyne then goes on to point out that Alex Tsakiris wasn't really interested in understanding the subject at hand but rather pushing his own particular agenda and in so doing neglecting to grasp even the basic fundamentals of evolutionary theory. In addition, it seems all too evident that Tsakiris is trying to make a name for himself by piggy backing on the stellar reputations of those he chooses to interview. He does this by his after-the-fact commentary that invariably highlights his own purview. While this is not surprising in itself (it is his own website, needless to say), Tsakiris' spin doesn't always do justice to those he interviews and thus oftentimes creates a false and misleading impression on his readers. As Coyne pointedly explained,

"The man has a habit of inserting his own summaries, recorded post facto, at the end and beginning of the podcast. That, of course, gives him the last say. Tsakiris was full of misconceptions about evolution—misconceptions to which he clung tenaciously. He was almost obsessed with the idea that Alfred Russel Wallace isn't just given too little credit for his contributions to evolutionary biology, but that he was in fact more important than Darwin in bringing about the acceptance of evolution. He was confused about group selection, which he sees as the reigning paradigm among evolutionists of how natural selection works. Tsakiris also wanted to talk about how quantum mechanics negates modern evolutionary theory, about the evils of materialism, about "quantum entanglement of neurons" (!) and about precognition. Anyway, I wasn't in any mood to put up with either woo or Alex's many distortions of evolutionary biology and its history, and I'm afraid I went a bit Hitchens on him. Too bad—but he deserved it. I hate it when hosts ask you on to talk about your field and then wind up using the discussion as a platform to expound their own ideas, especially when they're crazy ideas."

Outside of how we ultimately interpret Tsakiris' interview with Patricia Churchland, there is no doubt that NDE's and how we ultimately interpret them is a hugely controversial topic. There seems to be a deep resistance amongst many to a physical explanation for why extraordinary experiences happen near or at the time of death. Yet, as I have argued before in several essays, I think those positing a mystical worldview are actually much better off by encouraging scientists to continue looking for a purely physical causation behind NDE's. Why? Because if NDE's are truly trans-neuronal then researchers will inevitably uncover aspects which cannot be adequately explained by naturalistic methodologies. Thus, ironically, the empiricist ends up proffering more, not less, evidence for something transcendental. However, if we forego such a rationalist endeavor too early, then we run the very real risk of confusing a physical phenomenon with a spiritual one. In other words, I think it is wise to fully exhaust the brain-based possibilities for why NDE's may exist before prematurely theorizing about potential spiritual explanations.

To flesh this out in a more graphic, if slightly hyperbolic, example, I am reminded of an incident that happened to me last year when I riding my electric skateboard. As I was entering Mother's Beach, a park adjacent to where I live in Huntington Harbour, I tried to ride my board over a little bump only to find myself falling off and landing on my left elbow directly on the concrete sidewalk. I immediately knew something was wrong as I couldn't move my arm even a couple of inches. So, naturally, I went to the doctor who ordered an X-ray, but the film didn't reveal anything broken. However, he suggested that the X-ray might have missed something so he encouraged me to have an MRI, which I thankfully did, since it turned out that I did indeed have a broken elbow. I was out of surfing and skateboarding commission for 8 weeks after that.

I bring this example up because I think it serves as a good analogy for why it is important not to dismiss too early the viable idea that NDE's may be products of our own neuroanatomy. The brain is the most complex structure we have uncovered in the universe so far and neuroscience is still in its infancy in understanding precisely how its various neural components work and interact. As such, the brain consists of extremely subtle and intricate pathways that have yet to be completely understood.

If a broken elbow can go undetected by an X-ray, but can later show up with a more sophisticated MRI scan, it gives one pause about how much more we will understand about the brain when our technology exponentially advances so we may unlock hitherto unknown lines of communication.

This is not to say a priori, though, that NDE's are merely brain generated, but that we should be exceptionally cautious before succumbing to what Paul Kurtz rightly called the "transcendental temptation," whereby in our desire to support a mystical worldview we carelessly and hurriedly forego a more rationalist and grounded approach.

The good news in championing intertheoretic reductionism is that if NDE's really are glimpses of a spiritual afterlife, then our science will end up driving itself to the very brink of an epistemological cul de sac and in the process reveal that which cannot be explained away. In this way we should always keep an open mind to new data, even if we should also be highly skeptical at the same turn. As Patricia Churchland explained to Alex Tsakiris, "Well, I think there's certainly quite a bit of evidence that at least some near-death experiences have a neurobiological basis. Of course, we can't be sure about all of them. Maybe you had one that doesn't have a neurobiological basis."

The authors of *Loyalty to Your Soul: The Heart of Spiritual Psychology*, H. Ronald Hulnick and Mary R. Hulnick have been associated with John-Roger Hinkins for over three decades. Part of their dedication in the frontispiece of the book is to J.R., wherein they write "and to John-Roger, who turned my Self around and helped me find direction and inspiration in my life"—Ron and "and to John-Roger whose exampleship [sic] has informed my life"—Mary.

Since both authors readily admit their allegiance to John-Roger Hinkins and his teachings, much of their "spiritual psychology" is inspired directly by J.R. This is without a doubt the most troubling thing about the book and it begins on page 1.

In doing a review of their 215-page tome (with blank pages from 216 onwards with a header entitled "Notes," apparently designed for engaged readers to make jottings to themselves), I thought it might be useful to highlight certain sections which underlined the theme of their narrative and which also piqued my skepticism as I kept reading.

First, in the Preface to the book, Ron and Mary explain why they moved from a mainstream academic life to joining J.R.'s fledgling school, Koh-E-Nor. They recollect,

"We were married in January 1978, which unexpectedly resulted in our leaving the university [Note: they never identify the school in the book; *Wikipedia*, May 23, 2011, claims that they were at New Mexico State University]. I was being groomed to be the chair of the department, and it was simply not possible for a chair to have a spouse as a faculty member in the same department."

As an academic myself, and having taught in several colleges and universities in my career I was a bit surprised to learn about Hulnicks' dilemma since I know of several instances of where the chairperson of a department also had a spouse within the department. Right off the top of my head I can think of three examples which contravene Hulnicks' claim. Patricia Churchland, the eminent founder of Neurophilosophy and Professor of Philosophy at UCSD, was Chair of her department for several years, even though her husband Paul Churchland was a member of the same. A few buildings down from the Philosophy department at UCSD, my old professor, the late

Bennett Berger was Chair of the Sociology department even though his wife was also a professor in the same department. Additionally, my own wife, Dr. Andrea Diem-Lane and I are tenured professors in the same Philosophy department at Mt. San Antonio College. She was asked on several occasions by our Dean to run for Chairperson, but nobody ever mentioned that she couldn't because I was her husband in the same department.

I raise this issue since the Hulnicks' explanation for why they departed from the university (on the basis that a husband and wife couldn't be in the same department, if one had assumed Chair) at best needs more background information to be convincing and at worst rings hollow. Something seems missing in their explanation. Eventually, after a year off from work, they met with John-Roger and formalized their association with J.R.'s school, with the first class graduating with eleven students in 1982. In the 1990s the name was switched from *Koh-E-Nor* to the University of Santa Monica. While the school has been granted "Institutional Approval" it still lacks full educational accreditation according to outside sources.

The Hulnicks take their nightly dreams seriously and in the Preface indicate that the very basis of their present book commenced because of a vivid dream Ron had, "in which John-Roger handed him a book with the word Loyalties written on the cover. The implication was clear. When we spoke with John-Roger, he simply stated, 'That wasn't a dream.'"

The thesis of their entire book is nicely summarized by them in the paragraph that follows, "It contains many of the principles and some of the practices currently offered in the two year Master's degree Program in Spiritual Psychology at the University of Santa Monica, where I serve as Chief Academic Officer and Ron is President."

Essentially, the Hulnicks and by extension USM (or, should that order be reversed?), want to bring "spirituality" (or soul) back into psychology, focusing on spiritual principles which they believe underline an evolutionary basis of both life and understanding.

Now, much of their book has a series of nice platitudes that for the most part make for uplifting reading. In sum, they are trying to liberate individuals from a merely egoic viewpoint where one tends to see things only as "happening to me" versus taking responsibility for one's reactions which occur, they argue, always within one's self, regardless of uncontrollable outward events. On the surface, much of this terrain has been covered before by a host of New Age thinkers ranging from Deepak Chopra to John Bradshaw to Marilyn Ferguson and, to a lesser extent, Ken Wilber. The model they present is how one can move from a physical ego to a mental ego to an emotional ego to finally an "authentic" self, where unconditional love and acceptance reigns supreme. Much of this philosophy, of course, is in alignment with John-Roger spiritual teachings as displayed in his religious group, The Movement for Spiritual Inner Awareness (MSIA).

It is one of the great ironies of the book that the Hulnicks' speak repeatedly about transcending ego-based actions when their own spiritual teacher has demonstrated nothing of the sort. They write about "not judging" as if making such judgments were a hindrance to a truly liberated life. For instance, the Hulnicks' write, "You never did anything wrong but that you judged it as wrong."

While I can appreciate that on one level this might seem liberating, especially if one is racked by unnecessary guilt, but such a relativistic escape clause can also lead to excusing all sorts of reprehensible behavior. Indeed, there is dangerous duplicity with this New Age double-speak that too often boomerangs back upon the naïve believer who doesn't realize that making wise judgments in life is precisely how one avoids future pitfalls.

Peter McWilliams recounts a telling episode about the Hulnicks and how they responded when their dog bit Peter (drawing blood) at a dinner party at their house. It is both a funny and a revealing story:

"I had met Ron and Mary while they were still in New Mexico in 1979. They heard that I wrote books, they wanted to write books, so they invited me to dinner so they could talk about writing books. The Hulnicks had a big black pet--sort of a cross between a German shepherd, a black panther, and Jeffrey Dahmer. During dinner, the beast came up and bit me. I mean really bit me. Blood is dripping from my hand onto the glass-topped table. I am in pain. I have just been bitten by an animal of unknown origin, species, and cosmic influence. The Hulnicks cannot stop laughing. I show them: look, I am really bleeding. They laugh even harder. I say, I think I better get to a hospital. They think this is hilarious. They do absolutely nothing for me. They begin petting the beast and feeding it food from the table. I thought: 'Perhaps I am in a Stephen King novel--*PhiDo: The Flesh-Eating Mystery Animal of Higher Education*.' The dog started looking at me as though I were a Gainesburger. I knew what a can of Alpo felt like. I tried not to look afraid which no doubt is what those white mice try to do when they're placed in a cage of boa constrictors. I wrapped the napkin tightly around my hand, made some quick excuses, and got the hell out of there. As I drove away, I could hear Ron, Mary, and the beast laughing across the desert night. The next time I saw the Hulnicks was in Los Angeles about two years later. We said hello. I asked, 'How is the dog?' They said, 'It died.' I said, 'Good.' That effectively ended any hope for even a moderately cordial relationship between myself and Drs."

When the Hulnicks' spiritual guru was exposed in an extensive two-part feature in the *Los Angeles Times*, what was J.R.'s response? Instead of owning up to his many transgressions he deployed a bizarre subterfuge where he claimed to a live audience that "Roger" (the person responsible, but not admitting anything) had died and that only his pure self remained and that "the past was past." In addition, shortly before the Los Angeles Times story broke on August 14, 1988, John-Roger passed the keys of the Mystical Traveler over to John Morton, allegedly a one-time lover of J.R.'s and a close member of his personal staff. As Peter McWilliams recalls:

"Passing the keys to John Morton only a month before gave John-Roger one of his favorite defenses: evasive semantics. By passing the 'keys' to John Morton, John-Roger could answer, 'No,' to straightforward but perhaps embarrassing questions such as, 'Are you the Mystical Traveler?' . . . . It seemed as though John-Roger was denying he was ever the Traveler. It also allowed John-Roger to brush aside any questions of MSIA's past shady dealings with the comment, 'John Morton is in charge of MSIA; talk to him.'"

Indeed, John-Roger has had a long habit of avoiding taking responsibility for his actions. I remember confronting J.R. back in 1983 on the telephone over a laundry list of ethical transgressions. Not only did he deny that he ever did anything wrong, but he proceeded to terrorize those disciples of his that had defected.

It makes one wonder how the Hulnicks can with a straight face write an entire book about spiritual integrity when the very founder of their University has systematically avoided being held accountable for any of his actions, including such criminal activities as robbing a researcher's home and making death threats against defectors, as extensively detailed in the mid-1980s publication, *The Criminal Activities of John-Roger Hinkins*.

Or, do we tolerate such transgressions under New Age platitudes such as "don't engage in judging"? Isn't there something morally bankrupt in an ideology that allows the founder and spiritual guide of a University to avoid critical scrutiny by indulging in a form of semantic dodge ball?

The Hulnicks' message in *Loyalty to Your Soul* is about taking responsibility for one's life and actions, even under the most trying of circumstances. They write, "Within the spiritual context, you'd assume that you're responsible for everything in your life. However, you usually don't know the spiritual reason why your Soul would choose an experience such as cancer. What you do know is that all of life serves a spiritual purpose, and since illness is part of life, cancer must serve one, too."

Yet, curiously, they don't write extensively about taking responsibility for the harm one's actions can do to others, regardless of the right or wrong intentions behind them. They seem to be morally tone deaf when it comes to analyzing their own guru whose actions have caused deep and continuing turmoil in a number of his disaffected students.

Moreover, the very idea that our souls actually choose each and every event in our lives can at many turns legitimize unconscionable acts of depravity. Is it merely coincidental that such a theology permeates the University of Santa Monica when its very founder has indulged in all sorts of abusive interactions with those closest to him and those who would criticize him in public?

Furthermore, do the Hulnicks really believe that John-Roger, the founder and moral guide to USM, knows everything at all times? Because that is precisely what John-Roger has printed about himself. The 1979 edition of the MSIA Handbook for Ministers of Light states that "John-Roger Can See All. Remember, however, you might frighten a person in the beginning if you tell him John-Roger has the ability to know everything we're thinking and doing at all times. Though the person may not believe this at first, once he does start realizing it might true, he's apt to feel frightened."

Where is the accountability for such grandiose claims? As Carl Sagan often quipped (reformatting Laplace's earlier declaration): "Extraordinary claims demand extraordinary proof."

The Hulnicks, obviously following J.R.'s lead in this regard, make so many over-the-top claims in *Loyalty to Your Soul* that it becomes fairly obvious that much of what they write is more a religious theology (with a large number of untested claims) than a genuinely scientific primer on psychology.

For instance, the Hulnicks make such axiomatic claims as "The nature of God is Love," "Physical-world reality exists for the purpose of spiritual evolution," and "Since we are all part of God, our nature also is Love, and we have the opportunity to know our Loving nature experientially, here and now!" While no doubt one may wish to believe such niceties, the fact remains that such exclamations are religious in nature and indicate that the University of Santa Monica is more an extension of John-Roger's ministry than anything else.

As Peter McWilliams explains: "All of John-Roger's organizations have one of two functions: getting devotees for John-Roger or getting money from the devotees. USM does both. Based on the theory that if you hang around McDonald's long enough sooner or later you're going to have to have some fast food, if you hang around USM long enough, sooner or later you're going to join MSIA. Every staff person and most volunteers at USM are MSIA ministers and initiates. Ron Hulnick refers to USM within MSIA circles as 'the Traveler's School.'"

The unsuspecting student, not well versed in John-Roger's own peculiar blend of New Age thinking (mixing varying parts of Eckankar, Sant Mat, Theosophy, Christianity, EST, Lifespring, and whatever else captures J.R.'s interest at the moment), may enroll at the University of Santa Monica thinking that it is a purely secular school that is trying to incorporate tried and tested spiritual principles into its curriculum. But that is not the case at all, since the University of Santa Monica is, in truth, a fulcrum for John-Roger's idiosyncratic philosophy and, as such, serves as a potential vehicle for drawing new recruits into his own religious cult, MSIA.

In other words, if the University of Santa Monica (with the Hulnicks as Co-Directors of the Institution) was truthful in its advertising (and lived up to the intentions of its founder) and in its ultimate aims, then it might more appropriately bill itself as John-Roger U.

Do incoming students at USM know that the founder of the school advertises himself as "the one who can see and know all"? Do incoming students at USM know that John-Roger founded the school to promote his own self-styled theology? Do incoming students know that the creator of their university terrorized disciples in his entourage? That he allegedly engaged in numerous criminal activities, including robbery and death threats?

More pointedly, what does it say about the Hulnicks as educators that they have never criticized their school's founder and their personal spiritual teacher, John-Roger, for contradicting the integrity they so repeatedly advocate? John-Roger has demonstrated throughout his life that he lacks even the basic decency of a normal human being, much less the "soul" qualities that the Hulnicks advocate in their book.

Can a university built on the integrity of John-Roger Hinkins be trusted? Are students fully aware of what they are getting themselves into when they pay money to an organization that, on closer inspection, is a front for a cult theology? These and other questions are what incoming students need to answer before giving a dime to an institution that still lacks full educational accreditation.

In conclusion, perhaps the real lesson one can derive from the Hulnicks' book, *Loyalty to Your Soul,* is to realize that even highly educated counselors can be easily charmed and duped by the wiles of a manipulative cult leader who wants your ultimate loyalty not to be to yourself but to him. Just think: how did the founder of the University of Santa Monica respond when criticized? Did he admit to any wrongdoing? Did he seek forgiveness for past actions? Did he ever admit to do anything wrong? No. Instead John-Roger literally terrorized the lives of those who had shown the utmost loyalty to him. According to varying sources, he sued them. He robbed their homes. He threatened to kill them. One can only wonder aloud why anyone would want to attend a school founded by a man who once told his student, Peter McWilliams, who was dying from AIDS, that he would save him from death if he agreed to put John-Roger's name alongside his on future books. If one really wants to follow the moral injunctions of Hulnicks' book and be loyal to one's soul, it might be wise to read closely Peter McWilliams' book, *LIFE 102: What to Do When Your Guru Sues You,* which though no longer in print is still available in used editions from Amazon and other booksellers worldwide. Peter McWilliams unmasks the charade that is J.R. and in the process clearly explains why the University of Santa Monica should be better known as the University of Spiritual Manipulation.

POSTSCRIPT

Peter McWilliams recalls how Ron Hulnick responded to him after he left the University of Santa Monica and defected from John-Roger's cult:

"When Ron Hulnick first saw me pamphleting USM, he called me over in what seemed to be a conciliatory tone, and his first words were, 'If you set foot on our property, we're calling the police and having you arrested.'

In 1981, Koh-E-Nor University (John-Roger, founder and chancellor; Drs. Ron and Mary Hulnick, president and dean) was established. Koh-E-Nor means "mountain of light" or "mountain of wisdom" or "when you pile it this high and this deep, you get a mountain." The instant they were established, they started handing out honorary Ph.D.s. John-Roger got the first. He got an honorary doctorate in, I forget, but you can be sure that it was in anything he wanted. Russell Bishop got one. All the guys on staff got one. When John Morton got one, some people got suspicious about the university's academic standards: when accepting his honorary Ph.D. in (I think) nuclear physics, all John Morton could do was admire the wood grain. ("They did a really good job finishing this. Not too shiny.")

Suddenly, everybody at Insight had a Ph.D. The typesetters for the Insight brochures ran out of the letters P, h, and D. Facilitators actually started calling each/other "doctor"--and they weren't kidding! Not surprisingly, Russell was the worst. If you didn't call him "Dr. Bishop," he didn't answer. As far as Dr. Bishop was concerned, from now on "Russell" was what leaves did in the wind. Koh-E-Nor University opened its doors promising B.A.s, M.A.s, and Ph.D.s to one and all. "By the time you're done with the courses, we'll have full accreditation, and accreditation will be retroactive," it promised. But some things never change: as of August 1994, thirteen years later, J-R's University still isn't accredited, and Ron and Mary still don't like me."

In 1988, all the John-Roger organizations began a process John-Roger called "genetic cleansing." It was yet another prophylactic measure to protect "his babies" from the forthcoming Los Angeles Times article. All the organizations were told to change their names. This way, if the *L.A. Times* reported that one of the organizations had done something wrong, it wouldn't exist anymore. Only MSIA and Insight survived the purge: they had name-recognition and therefore there was money in them there names. Every other organization changed. The John-Roger Foundation and Integrity Institute became the Institute for Individual and World Peace; PRANA Theological Seminary became Peace Theological Seminary; Atman Travel became Esprit Travel; ACE became Educare; and Koh-E-Nor University became the University of Santa Monica. It was purely a random coincidence that one of the more respected community colleges in the state of California is called Santa Monica College. Could some people possibly think that Santa Monica College grew up and became a university? No. Nobody could make that kind of mistake. And if they did, they would get a far better education at the University of Santa Monica than they would at Santa Monica College. In connection with this name change, the Baraka Center for Holistic Health and Research became the University of Santa Monica Center for Health. The University of Santa Monica has classes one weekend a month. A school year is nine weekends over a nine-month period. There is no hope that they will ever get full accreditation. Still, the promises continue. Even the use of the word university to describe an institution that offers only two or three classes per semester is beyond me. Here's how the New American Heritage Dictionary defines university: "An institution for higher learning with teaching and research facilities comprising a graduate school and professional schools that award master's degrees and doctorates and an undergraduate division that awards bachelor's degrees". The only degrees USM students get are the ones they came in with, and-other than answering the burning question: "How many years can we get away with charging money for degrees the students never get?" In 1994, USM made a splashy announcement when they were finally accredited by the Pacific Association of Schools and Colleges (PASC). Other institutes of higher learning accredited by PASC include acupuncture schools, massage schools, herbal schools, and other New Age learning centers. Now, if the Pacific Association of Schools and Colleges can only get accredited by the U.S. Department of Education, USM can hand out genuine Ph.D.s!

USM announced that PASC's accreditation is imminent! How exciting! John-Roger agrees to do a fundraising seminar! Seventy-five dollars per person! All money going to PASC's Accreditation Fund! It looks as though one of John-Roger's institutions will actually keep its word (thirteen years later, but, hey, what the heck?)! Knowing that John-Roger's organizations don't always tell the full story of what's going on, I wrote to the U.S. Department of Education inquiring about the University of Santa Monica and the Pacific Association of Schools and Colleges. In a letter to me, Carl S. Person, chief of the Accrediting Agency of the Evaluation Branch of the Department of Education, wrote on July 25, 1994: The University of Santa Monica had contacted the Pacific Association of Schools and Colleges (PASC) concerning possible accreditation. At that time, PASC had been petitioning the Secretary of Education for listing as a nationally recognized accrediting agency. Since the regulations for recognizing accrediting agencies have recently changed, PASC withdrew its petition before any final decision was made.

The organization that accredited USM, then, doesn't even have an application on file to receive accreditation from the U.S. Department of Education. Meanwhile, on August 19, 1994, John-Roger still did a fundraising seminar. Nowhere in the advertisements promoting this fundraising event does it say that PASC is about as close to being accredited as, oh, my publishing company, Prelude Press. That John-Roger would continue with a fundraiser for what appears to be a lost cause is nothing new. He has raised money for one project after another, and when the project failed to materialize, there wasn't a hint of refunding any money. There was never even a letter saying where the money would go instead.

I spent a school year at USM once. For nine excruciatingly dull weekends, I suffered through the boredom of the program the Hulnicks had created, and, for a change of pace, the boredom of the Hulnicks themselves. Dear God, it was painful. Somewhere early on in the nine-month process, I came to believe that I was sexually addicted. With the full support and encouragement of the University of Santa Monica staff, volunteers, and students, I spent the next eight months without having so much as an orgasm. Through total abstinence, Ron and Mary said, my addictive patterns concerning sex were supposed to "come up." I think I am going to leave this paragraph now, because with that last sentence I am no longer safe here. Sometime around month eight, I saw an ad for a lecture by Dr.

Albert Ellis. (The lecture was not connected to USM). I was thrilled. I, along with about eight hundred other Los Angelenos, filled a ballroom one Friday evening. Dr. Ellis spoke for awhile, which was a treat, and then he offered to demonstrate how swift and effective his technique of Rational-Emotive Therapy can be. He invited anyone courageous enough to sit in the chair next to him, explain his or her biggest problem, and Dr. Ellis would use Rational-Emotive Therapy to solve it. He was spectacular.

He knocked off problems left and right. You name it; he fixed it-and they seemed to me good fixes, too. In fifteen to twenty minutes each, the people were on their way with a new view of life. When it was my turn, I sat down and told Dr Ellis—and assembled masses–that I was sexually addicted.

"How do you know that you are sexually addicted?" Dr. Ellis asked. "Well, in the eight months since I've had an orgasm, what's come up is … ," I began. "You haven't had an orgasm in eight months?" You could see Dr. Ellis was a believer in Remy de Gourmont's philosophy: "Of all sexual aberrations, perhaps the most peculiar is chastity." "Yes," I said sheepishly. "Maybe it was only seven months and three weeks." "You're not sexually addicted!" proclaimed Dr. Ellis. "If you had a sexual addiction you couldn't possibly go eight months without an orgasm. The fact that you went eight months without an orgasm proves conclusively that you're not sexually addicted." Wow. I had spent eight months at USM looking for the causes of my sexual addiction, but no one thought to ask whether or not I was sexually addicted in the first place. In the pseudo-mezzo spiritual atmosphere of USM, any sexual attraction seemed marginally perverse. Around USM, even sex within marriage seemed somehow, well, distracting.

Ron and Mary did not exactly celebrate the joys of the physical union in either discussion or demeanor: it was somehow difficult to imagine that they ever actually "did it." It was like trying to imagine your parents doing it when you first found out all parents did it. Thanks to USM's psychological (pathological?) hang-up concerning sex, I spent eight months looking for the cause of a problem I didn't have. Dr. Ellis was right; his logic impeccable. Once again–as in 1965– was saved by the good doctor.

All of John-Roger's organizations have one of two functions: getting devotees for John-Roger or getting money from the devotees. USM does both. Based on the theory that if you hang around McDonald's long enough sooner or later you're going to have to have some fast food, if you hang around USM long enough, sooner or later you're going to join MSIA. Every staff person and most volunteers at USM are MSIA ministers and initiates. Ron Hulnick refers to USM within MSIA circles as "the Traveler's School."

My Association with Peter McWilliams

I first became aware of Peter McWilliams when I saw him trying to prevent Craig Rivera (Geraldo's younger brother) from filming John-Roger Hinkins at a book signing. The clip was repeatedly shown on Geraldo Rivera's early 1990s nightly news television show, Now It Can Be Told, which devoted an entire episode on J.R. infamously entitled "The Cadillac of Cults." I also appeared on that show discussing how J.R. had ransacked my home and how J.R. had manipulated hundreds of his disciples with his false claims.

Later in the summer of 1994 I was quite surprised to receive an urgent phone call from Peter McWilliams asking me for my help. I was traveling through Austin, Texas, at the time and he wanted to meet me personally as soon as possible. A week or so later we met in Del Mar, California (where I was then living) at Il Fornaio, an Italian restaurant.

Peter explained that he had defected from MSIA and that he wanted to write a book exposing his former guru but in order to do so he needed my help. I explained that I was hesitant to put my neck out again, since the last time I wrote about J.R. I got death threats and got my home robbed. In addition, I wanted to make absolutely certain that Peter was going to put his name front and center on his critical analysis, since I had previously noted a tendency among certain MSIA defectors of running scared (out of fear of J.R.'s possible reprisals) when their names were going to be published as key sources.

I liked Peter almost immediately. He was very bright and exceptionally witty. He described in detail how manipulated he felt under J.R.'s tutelage. Although Peter listed John-Roger as a co-author to his very successful Life 101 book series, he stressed to me that John-Roger hadn't actually written anything in his books.

As Peter later explained, "I put his name on books I wrote, including *Life 101, DO IT!,* and *You Can't Afford the Luxury of a Negative Thought....* I published and promoted the books myself and two of them appeared on the New York Times bestseller list. I gave John-Roger every spare penny the books generated— more than 1,000,00... I did all of this not from love, but fear: I thought if I didn't, I would die. I actually believed John-Roger's lies that h was keeping me alive."

I decided to give Peter McWilliams all the files, articles, tapes, and assorted papers I had on J.R., including some very personal items which clearly showed that the founder of MSIA was involved in criminal activities.

I conversed with Peter several more times during that month on the phone, through slow and electronic mail, and personally.

He finished his magnus opus on John-Roger, *What To Do When Your Guru Sues You*, in record time. It still remains one of the most insightful and funny portraits of a cult leader ever written.

The book had an almost immediate impact, as the national press soon learned that Arianna Huffington was a long-time associate of J.R. and an ordained minister in the Movement, a point that she tried to vehemently deny on T.V. But Arianna's less than truthful responses about her J.R. connection turned out to have a devastating impact on her husband's senatorial campaign. Some analysts have argued that *Life 102* actually transformed the political outcome of the race, as Michael Huffington only lost the election by less than two percent of the vote to incumbent Diane Feinstein. Having his wife exposed on two fronts (denying her obvious association John-Roger and employing an illegal immigrant) just weeks before the general election cost Michael Huffington a number of key swing votes. Not long thereafter, Michael and Arianna were divorced and today Michael Huffington has declared that he is bisexual.

Life 102 was widely distributed throughout North America and was featured on a number of radio and television programs. Peter also did extensive interviews promoting the book. It caused a tremendous controversy in MSIA since it contained explosive allegations about J.R. and his nefarious activities with his closest disciples and those who have publicly criticized him.

Life 102 was readily available for several years after its initial publication in the Fall of 1994. However, J.R waged an intense legal battle against Peter McWilliams in the ensuing years and this took a dramatic toll on Peter's health.

In late 1996 while I was living in London, England, on sabbatical, I received a shocking phone call from a friend of mine who informed me that Peter McWilliams had brokered a deal with J.R.'s organization to sell all of the rights to *Life 102* over to MSIA in exchange for 2 million dollars cash. I was flabbergasted. I couldn't believe that Peter would cave in to J.R. after all the pain and turmoil he had been put through because of John-Roger's lies and deceit. But it was a done deal. The very object of Peter McWilliams' critique (J.R.) now owned the rights to the book that had so brilliantly exposed him as charlatan. J.R. and MSIA had all the copies of *Life 102* pulled and sent out letters requesting that any and all electronic versions of the book also be taken down from websites that hosted them.

I had made a deal with Peter very early on in our negotiations back in 1994 that if I was going to help him on his project that I would be given his permission to post the book, *Life 102*, on my website for free so that any interested seeker or scholar could have access to it.

What I hadn't ever imagined was that in the not so distant future Peter McWilliams would sell back his book to John-Roger. This put me in an awfully precarious position since my website was the last place on the Internet that still displayed an unedited version of *Life 102*.

I was a sitting duck, since I refused to take the book down. I soon heard from MSIA's lawyer requesting that I take the book off my Neuralsurfer website immediately. I refused to do so and got legal representation to argue for my position.

What was MSIA's reaction to my perhaps naïve refusal to cow tow to their demands? They sued me. At that stage I was uncertain about what to do since I had already had a number of ugly legal skirmishes with another new religious movement, Eckankar, which I had written extensively about. I was gun shy since I already knew from past experiences that legal tussles usually turn out worse than expected. However, my lawyers were convinced that I had a strong case, especially since Peter McWilliams had written the following to me:

David-
Tada! Here it is in print form — Life 102! Let me know if you need more. Thank you for all your help. I couldn't have done it without you. Yes, of course, put it on your web page, give copies to your class. Whatever you want – just don't sell it. Again, thanks I owe you several! Enjoy–Peter McWilliams, 9/94.

Eventually lawyers on both sides deposed Peter and me. After Peter's deposition which my lawyers felt fully backed my position, MSIA attempted to settle the impending case with me out of court. They even offered me some modest compensation but under the stipulation that I had to agree to take *Life 102* off my website. My lawyers recommended that I refuse the offer and let the issue go to trial. I was hesitant to do so because I knew that I might end up losing the case, since Peter had legally transferred his rights to the book over to J.R. and MSIA.

The strength of my case rested on the fact that I only agreed to help Peter write his book if I was allowed permission to post the entire book on my newly created website, the Neuralsurfer. The case would make or break on the veracity of Peter's testimony, as he was my sole witness at the trial.

However, something totally unexpected happened just days before the case went to trial. Peter McWilliams was arrested by the Federal Government for growing marijuana illegally. Shortly after leaving John-Roger, Peter learned that he had AIDS and that the medicine he was prescribed to take was extremely difficult to swallow without him getting nauseous. To counteract the nausea and vomiting he discovered that smoking pot helped him to hold down his necessary medicines. He became a champion for medical marijuana since he knew how much it had helped him.

But the Federal Government didn't agree with Peter's outspoken advocacy and arrested him for illegally growing and distributing marijuana. Peter was put into jail and was not allowed to take his AIDS medicine for several days. This naturally caused him to become quite ill. On the day of the trial, the judge was informed that our witness was in Federal custody and therefore couldn't appear as my expert witness. The judge, however, ordered that Peter McWilliams be taken from jail in shackles and brought into the courtroom to testify.

The moment I saw Peter shuffling into the courtroom with his haggard appearance I knew I had lost the case. The fact that Peter walked by my lawyer and me and winked in full view of the judge didn't help matters either.

Peter tried his best to convince the judge that I had a prior right to post the book on my website and that such a right preceded the agreement he had made with MSIA. But to no avail. The judge ruled against me and I was ordered to take the book off my website. Although Peter testified at the trial that he had indeed given me a prior license for posting *Life 102* on my website (As the judge admitted in her judgment "Despite his representation and warranty that he has not assigned or granted any license in *Life 102* for consideration, McWilliams testified at trial that he advised representatives of MSIA at the time of the settlement that he had previously granted a license for consideration to use *Life 102* to Lane.") the judge ruled that she didn't find such testimony credible, primarily because Peter and his lawyer had given conflicting statements in other contexts.

I was, to say the least, flabbergasted. Peter was also exceptionally distraught about the outcome, since he knew that by selling back his copyright to MSIA he had put me (once again?) in a vulnerable position to the very person who had allegedly threatened my wife's life, ransacked my home, and staged a smear campaign against me and my informants from exposing the underside of John-Roger and his operations. A few months later, *Skeptic Magazine* published a brief notice on the trial and commented on how they thought the outcome was unfair and unwarranted.

The following year (1999) on my birthday, April 29th, I got an unexpected phone call from Peter McWilliams. He was trying to broker a truce between me and MSIA (or more specifically, John-Roger Hinkins). He knew that I was thinking of writing a follow-up study on John-Roger (which I had tentatively entitled Life 103: John-Roger against Me). However, my own personal and professional life was such that I wanted to avoid any further litigation with the already litigiously minded cult. So, eventually, a deal was hammered out with the President of MSIA and me to mitigate the bad blood that had percolated for some fifteen years.

To partly accomplish that aim MSIA invited Dr. J. Gordon Melton, head of the Institute for the Study of American Religion (and an old friend of mine and a sympathetic scholar to emerging new religions like MSIA) to meet with me at the University of Santa Monica to go over some of my past history with MSIA and to partly bury the hatchet. If I remember correctly, the President of MSIA had the interview filmed for posterity's sake. However, instead of reconciliation, my discussion with Dr. Melton increasingly focused on how I believed John-Roger robbed my home and how he had orchestrated a terror campaign out of a phony front organization called the *Coalition for Civil and Spiritual Rights* (CCSR). Right in the middle of the discussions, Dr. Melton and I realized that the P.O. Box that was used to send out CCSR's missives was just a few blocks down the street from the University of Santa Monica.

Looking at Dr. Melton's chagrined face that day made me think that he too realized how culpable John-Roger had been in smearing his defectors. It came as no surprise to me to learn later that MSIA didn't release the taped interview of Melton and

106

myself at USM to the public. Why should they? It mostly shows me explaining how badly J.R. reacts to criticism.

While my life trajectory, and apparently that of John-Roger's as well, took a turn for the better during the next year, the same cannot be said for Peter McWilliams. The very next year Peter died. It was a death many observers believe could have been prevented if the Federal Government would have listened to Peter McWilliams' plea for help.

As the late conservative commentator, William F. Buckley lamented, "Age? Fifty. Profession? Author, poet, publisher. Particular focus of interest? A federal judge in California (George King) would decide in a few weeks how long a sentence to hand down, and whether to send McWilliams to prison or let him serve his sentence at home. What was his offense? He collaborated in growing marijuana plants. What was his defense? Well, the judge wouldn't allow him to plead his defense to the jury. If given a chance, the defense would have argued that under Proposition 215, passed into California constitutional law in 1996, infirm Californians who got medical relief from marijuana were permitted to use it. The judge also forbade any mention that McWilliams suffered from AIDS and cancer, and got relief from the marijuana. What was he doing when he died? Vomiting. The vomiting hit him while in his bathtub, and he choked to death. Was there nothing he might have done to still the impulse to vomit? Yes, he could have taken marijuana; but the judge's bail terms forbade him to do so, and he submitted to weekly urine tests to confirm that he was living up to the terms of his bail. Did anybody take note of the risk he was undergoing? He took Marinol — a proffered, legal substitute, but reported after using it that it worked for him only about one-third of the time. When it didn't work, he vomited. Was there no public protest against the judge's ruling? Yes. On June 9, the television program 20/20 devoted a segment to the McWilliams plight. Commentator John Stossel summarized: 'McWilliams is out of prison on the condition that he not smoke marijuana, but it was the marijuana that kept him from vomiting up his medication. I can understand that the federal drug police don't agree with what some states have decided to do about medical marijuana, but does that give them the right to just end-run those laws and lock people up?' Shortly after the trial last year, Charles Levendosky, writing in the Ventura County (Calif.) Star, summarized: 'The cancer treatment resulted in complete remission.' But only the marijuana gave him sustained relief from the vomiting that proved mortal. Is it being said, in plain language, that the judge's obstinacy resulted in killing McWilliams? Yes. A Libertarian Party press release has made exactly that charge. 'McWilliams was prohibited from using medical marijuana–and being denied access to the drug's anti-nausea properties almost certainly caused his death.' Reflecting on the judge's refusal to let the jury know that there was understandable reason for McWilliams to believe he was acting legally, I ended a column in November by writing, 'So, the fate of Peter McWilliams is in the hands of Judge King. Perhaps the cool thing for him to do is delay a ruling for a few months, and just let Peter McWilliams die.' Well, that happened on June 14. The struggle against a fanatical imposition of federal laws on marijuana will continue, as also on the question whether federal laws can stifle state initiatives. Those who believe the marijuana laws are insanely misdirected have a martyr."

CONCLUDING REMARKS

In conclusion I should point out one of the very kind things Peter McWilliams did near the last year of his life. Because he felt badly about how the legal case against me turned out, Peter did all that he could to rectify the situation, including issuing statements that would help set up a relative truce between me and John-Roger.

Although it is widely reported that Peter somehow repudiated the findings of *Life 102* (as it states in the Wikipedia entry on him, dated June 7, 20012, "The content of the book is no longer one with which I would like to have my name associated."), I know from my personal conversations with him that Peter issued that statement in part to help insure that John-Roger and I could reach some sort of peace agreement. The truth of the matter is that Peter had become completely disillusioned with religion in general and as such didn't see MSIA as all that different from Roman Catholicism, since both of them believed in things that he thought were at best silly and at worst downright horrific. As I recalled in a brief piece I wrote about Peter's later theological views near the end of this life, God 101: There is None?

"However, before my case went to trial I got the chance to meet Peter again in his Hollywood home (which he had bought with his new found wealth). He was chain-smoking pot and had his pool in the dead of winter heated to about 100 degrees. He greeted me at the door with a bird on his shoulder wearing nothing but a bathrobe and a reefer dangling out of his mouth. We discussed many things that night (which, again, I hope to retell in more detail in a different article), but one thing he said has always stuck with me. Peter mentioned that he wanted to write a final book in his Life 101 series that had made him and J.R. relatively famous since they sold hundreds of thousands of copies.

Peter had been deeply involved with mystical traditions for decades (he once wrote a very popular treatise on Maharishi Mahesh Yogi and T.M.) and felt that they were completely wrong. Indeed, he changed from becoming an extremely devoted believer to a rabid skeptic of anything smacking of religion. He wanted to call his new book, God 101: There is None. Peter, as far I know, never finished that book because his life was cut short when he was forced by the Feds to stop his intake of medical marijuana, the one substance that he found that could control his nausea after taking his AIDS medicine.

Without the pot, he couldn't hold down his prescribed medicines. I can personally vouch for this since I saw Peter 's condition when he was in jail without pot and when he was at his home with an abundant supply. In any case, Peter chided me on my persistent agnostic-mystic leanings (as I tell my students at CSULB and MSAC, when they ask me about my religious tendencies, 'I am just too stupid to be a full-fledged atheist'), and tried to convince me that the only real enlightenment to be had was through hemp! I have always had a fondness for Peter, even if at one-time I was aghast that he compromised so many of his informants, including me, by selling *Life 102* to J.R.

However, I too have found myself in compromising positions (where I made my own bargains with the Devil) and one can quite understand how two million dollars cash can be a persuasive dealmaker. Peter McWilliams, I believe, would have written one of the best atheist books in the past twenty years if he had lived long enough. He could have given Richard Dawkins, Christopher Hitchens, and Sam Harris a serious run for their money, primarily because Peter would have written a genuinely funny book on why he and everyone else shouldn't believe in God.

Peter McWilliams on John-Roger as Thief

"In 1983, several of the people who left MSIA (one John-Roger's personal secretary, another a member of John-Roger's live-in personal staff) were tired of the intimidation, threats, and harassment, and also felt that the hidden story about John-Roger's evil empire needed to be told. They contacted Professor David Lane, Ph.D., who had written a book, The Making of a Spiritual Movement, which conclusively proved that the teachings of Eckankar came from the Radhasoami tradition of India. The book rocked the Eckankar organization to its very foundation. (Or, if you prefer, rocked the Eckankar foundation to its very organization.) Dr. Lane had also met with John-Roger on several occasions, and they were on friendly terms. To the former staff members, Dr. Lane seemed to be the ideal choice to investigate and report on what had been carefully hidden within John-Roger's organizations: he was an academician with a commitment to truth and a knowledge of spiritual practices (he himself follows a spiritual path) that would allow him to distinguish between legitimate spiritual teaching and the illegitimate-sometimes outrageous-justifications in the name of God given by John-Roger.

Dr. Lane's casual but cordial relationship with John-Roger would eliminate any basis for the charge that Dr. Lane had intentionally set out to do a hatchet job. After doing some preliminary research, Dr. Lane found that, although he was certainly shocked by what he discovered, he was somehow not inclined to complete the project. Dr. Lane was on the verge of abandoning his article when John-Roger- who shoots himself in the foot so often he should wear stainless steel socks-began harassing Dr. Lane. Wrong move. Dr. Lane, as he had proved when he took on the entire Eckankar organization (far larger than MSIA) did not succumb to intimidation. The fact that John-Roger was so eager to keep Dr. Lane from exploring any further indicated that there was good exploration ahead. In mid-1984, he published The J.R. Controversy: A Critical Analysis of John-Roger Hinkins and M.S.I.A. This article, published in Dr. Lane's research series "Understanding Cults and Spiritual Movements," was a breakthrough work on exposing the dark side of John-Roger's farce. The article revealed and documented for the first time John-Roger's plagiarism, intimidation, violence, and sexual exploits.

John-Roger's response? A general denial of the facts, and a general attack on Dr. Lane. On October 5, 1984, having driven to Del Mar, California, in John-Roger's baby-blue Lincoln Continental, John-Roger and Michael Feder broke into Dr. Lane's apartment in Del Mar, California. John-Roger is placed at the scene of the crime because of two words he wrote on a box containing copies of The].R. Controversy. The words were: "NO MORE." Handwriting experts have verified that this was written in John-Roger's hand, and it fits John-Roger's pattern of not being able to resist having the last word or to add a didactic comment to every situation.

By writing "NO MORE" on a box containing The J.R. Controversy, he did both. Michael Feder was placed in the apartment because the bed was turned completely over, a physical feat John-Roger would have been incapable of doing alone. Only John Roger and Michael Feder made the trip (they told the other staff members they were going to San Diego. It is possible that John-Roger left Michael Feder behind and picked up another henchman in Del Mar, but considering Michael Feder's ongoing shady doings with John-Roger, Feder is the most likely suspect. In addition to the bed's being turned over, the entire apartment was ransacked. To make absolutely certain that Dr. Lane would not think common, garden-variety thieves had broken in, the television, stereo, and other valuables were not taken. What was taken was Dr. Lane's years of research on spiritual groups and cults-the files on MSIA and Eckankar in particular. Also taken were two personal diaries written by Dr. Lane's wife, Jacquie; the list of subscribers for Dr. Lane's research series "Understanding Cults and Spiritual Movements," Dr. Lane's briefcase containing uncorrected term papers ("to the chagrin of my college students," notes Dr. Lane), and a card file containing a lifetime of Dr. Lane's collected recipes . The latter was "a heavy blow for me," remembers Dr. Lane, "the robbers probably thought it contained secret, inside information and thus was done in code."

It was not immediately clear who took the materials- it could have been someone from MSIA, or it could have been someone from Eckankar, from one of the other cults Dr. Lane was researching, or someone who gets off on reading the diaries of college professors' wives. The police, with so many possible culprits, were unable to act. Over the next year (which we shall explore next), as the information implicating John-Roger

111

gradually appeared, the handwriting analysis of "NO MORE" confirmed John-Roger's physical participation in the robbery

With the robbery, John-Roger's work was far from done. He began writing letters to Dr. Lane's spiritual teacher in India, referring to stolen documents and intimate entries in Dr. Lane's wife's diary: These were sent under an assumed name, but all came from the same printer connected to John-Roger's Lisa computer locked in a room in Mandeville Canyon to which only John-Roger and Michael Feder had the key. John-Roger must have supposed that Dr. Lane's spiritual teacher was the same sort of vindictive rumor-mongering, petty person as John-Roger. (Tattletale letters–many anonymous—are rampant in MSIA. And John-Roger loves them. The rules of evidence don't apply around John-Roger: however information is obtained is fair game.)

Fortunately, Dr. Lane's spiritual teacher was genuinely spiritual: his only response was to forward the letters that John-Roger had penned over any number of names along with a note saying simply; "I see no reason to do anything about these." Dr. Lane's spiritual teacher did not even give John-Roger's nonsense the dignity of a response. And a response was possible: John-Roger gave his post office box just in case Dr. Lane's spiritual teacher had a little dirt to share about some of John-Roger's disciples. The international spiritual kaffeeklatsch envisioned by John-Roger never materialized. Using the same post office box, John-Roger began an organization entitled (get this) Coalition for Civil and Spiritual Rights. That John-Roger would start a campaign for civil rights is so heavy with irony that I can't even get it off the ground with a good metaphor. The only civil rights John-Roger cares about- like all the great autocratic rulers before him- are his own. And spiritual rights? Well, John-Roger likes to use the word spiritual, and he always needs to be right, but that's about the closest connection I can make to the term "spiritual rights" and John-Roger Hinkins. The Coalition for Civil and Spiritual Rights was, of course, an organization with a good-sounding name that allowed John-Roger to pretend Dr. Lane was attacking John-Roger's religious freedom.

Never mind that he wanted the freedom to pass himself off as the one and only person on earth directly connected to God, as well as the civil rights to manipulate others unscrupulously; without being subject to criticism or external control. John-Roger, of course, did not step forth to defend himself: he created a triumvirate of characters (Michael Hunt, Kip Ferguson–a character he no doubt stole from one of his gay pulp porn novels—the distinguished Peter Davidson, Ph.D.). These three defended John-Roger's position with all the sophistication and elan of Ruby of Orange County. Fortunately (again), the Coalition for Civil and Spiritual Rights—which John-Roger no doubt envisioned as his own personal Moral Majority–never got off the ground. (Too heavy with irony; as you will recall.)

John-Roger also sent a 28-page, single-spaced letter (probably written by Michael Feder with John-Roger's comments) to Dr. Lane's professors (he was working on his doctorate), employers, and members of the spiritual and psychological intellectual community. By November of 1985, John-Roger had had just about as much fun with Dr. Lane as he (John-Roger) could tolerate. He packed up a good cross-section of the purloined Dr. Lane research materials, threw in Dr. Lane's wife's diaries for good measure, and sent the whole thing anonymously to Eckankar headquarters. Since all the' materials sent either directly related to Dr. Lane's Eckankar research, Dr. Lane's informants, or possibly embarrassing information about Dr. Lane (his recipe for Del Mar Lentil Loaf is positively scandalous), John-Roger assumed the Eckankar people, who had previously been reported on by Dr. Lane, would take over where John-Roger left off. More torment for Dr. Lane. Good. But there was something even better: if the Eckankar organization began using information from the robbery in its own smear campaign, the robbery would then be traced to Eckankar and not to John-Roger. It seemed a brilliant move: kill two birds plus crush every egg in the nest with one exceedingly large stone.

Brilliant, brilliant! Destroy his competition (Eckankar) and his critic (Dr. Lane) with one well-placed box of papers. Alas, John-Roger's Wile E. Coyote complex once again raised its weary head. Just as M. Coyote shoves a stick of dynamite down Roadrunner's throat, only to find it explodes in his own butt, JohnRoger's best-planted bombs often wind up exploding in his own face. In this case, the Eckankar people opened the box, and sent it directly to their lawyers; the lawyers immediately placed the entire box in another box and sent it to David Lane. By this point, David Lane was entirely certain that John-Roger was not only the thief, but also the mastermind and head writer (why didn't John-Roger spend all that writing time working on a book such as Petulance 101?) behind the smear campaign.

Also in the box of materials returned by John-Roger (by way of Eckankar), was, as Dr. Lane puts it, "cherry on the sundae." In the margins of Dr. Lanes wife's diary were handwritten comments. Handwriting experts venfled that this was the handwriting of . . . Beep beep."

THE J.R. CONTROVERSY
A Critical Analysis of John-Roger Hinkins and M.S.I.A.

[Written in 1983/1984 and published in Understanding Cults and Spiritual Movements]

What would you do if you learned one day that your spiritual teacher sexually harassed his male disciples and covered up his sexual affairs; a plagiarist who lifted his teachings from other traditions without due reference; a spendthrift who lived extravagantly, though he took a vow of poverty; a questionable business man who engaged in risky and possibly illegal activities; and a religious charlatan who consistently told untruths about a variety of issues?

Break-off your discipleship? Leave the organization? Stay with the movement? How would you feel? Shocked, disgusted, saddened? Or, perhaps, a strong sense of rationalization: okay, he may be sexually manipulative, a plagiarist, a crook, and a liar, but I have benefitted from him spiritually!

Right now this is the dilemma of several members of M.S.I.A. (Movement of Spiritual Inner Awareness) who believe that their teacher John-Roger has misled them and thousands of others. Based primarily upon the personal testimony of disciples of John-Roger about his hidden life, a scandal of devastating proportions has begun to rock the Movement's international membership. This article, the first of its kind, will take a close look at the present controversy, addressing the larger issue of how new religious groups should be studied in light of legitimacy and authenticity.

The Critical Imperative: Legitimacy versus Authenticity

With the continuing growth of new spiritual movements, it is imperative for both the scholar and the seeker to be able to discriminate between groups that are fraudulent and manipulative and those that are genuine and beneficial. The failure to do so has troublesome consequences: witness Jim Jones and Jonestown. What is necessary, therefore, in the examination of religion and its mystical claims–be them old and traditional

114

like Roman Catholicism or new and emerging like the Unification Church–is unbridled rational scrutiny. That is, the opportunity to fully investigate every facet about the particular spiritual movement: from the biography of its founder, the history of its organization, the value of its teachings, to the practical application of its techniques, etc. Nothing, in this purview, is too private, too esoteric, or too trivial for examination.

However, some of today's religions resist such inquiries, fearing the negative repercussions that may result from an intensive study of their history and doctrines. For instance, note the reluctance of many followers to accept historians' allegations that many esteemed religious leaders plagiarized their writings from other authors, e.g., Joseph Smith (Mormonism) and Mary Baker Eddy (Christian Science).

Though we may indeed find many unpleasant facts out about the originators and promulgators of spiritual movements, this does not in any way lessen our responsibility to uncover the truth (in whatever form it may appear). This above all else is the rational imperative and the duty of human intelligence: to question and probe unceasingly.

Ken Wilber, perhaps more than any other transpersonal theorist, has stressed the need for intelligent discrimination in the face of our modern cultic renaissance. In his books, *A Sociable God* (1983) and *Eye to Eye* (1983), Wilber has proposed a simple but dynamic paradigm in which to critically analyze new religious movements.[1]

Borrowing his terminology from linguistics and sociology, Wilber argues that spiritual groups should be judged on two criteria: legitimacy and authenticity. The former deals with the relative degree of meaning value found in the group. How well do its teachings integrate one within both the membership fold and the exterior community? Does the leader/teacher live up to his/her own ethical standards? To the moral heights of other enlightened masters? What are the group's historical antecedents? How is it viewed by outsiders, etc.? Legitimacy is a horizontal enterprise, the valuation of the movement's aims within the individual, membership, and the society at large.

Authenticity, on the other hand, is concerned with the actual transformation offered and delivered by the respective sect. Is the group engaged with transcendent practices for uplifting the soul to higher realms? Or, just the alteration of social and political awareness? Are participants experiencing directly those desired aims, etc.? This, as Huston Smith in The Forgotten Truth has pointed out, is a vertical appraisement, gauging the spiritual focus and power of the movement both theoretically and practically.

With Wilber's astute reconnoitering of religious groups, it will enable us to examine John-Roger and M.S.I.A. more fully, taking into consideration both the integrative and transformative dimensions of his group.

A Brief History of M.S.I.A.

In 1968 John-Roger Hinkins, reportedly a former police dispatcher and ex-high school teacher raised in Mormonism, started his spiritual ministry in California. He was associated with Paul Twitchell and his group, having been a mail correspondent member and a second initiate.[2] There are also reports that he was connected with other metaphysical groups, learning firsthand about meditation, light-attunement, and aura balancing,[3] which he later incorporated into his own movement.

Although Hinkins' name appears in Twitchell's newsletter (dated in the late 1960's) as a convener for Twitchell sponsored meetings in Southern California, John-Roger does not see his connection with Paul Twitchell as a master/disciple or teacher/student relationship. Be that as it may, the fact remains, however, that his group and his teachings are almost exactly the same as those taught by Paul Twitchell, not even excepting particular Twitchellian nuances.[4] Likewise, some M.S.I.A. initiates recall that in the early meetings J.R. would "call in" the spirit of brother Paul Twitchell, as a master conversant in soul travel. It should also be recognized that M.S.I.A.'s organizational structure is almost parallel to Twitchell's group with regard to initiation, discourses, and cosmology.[5]

John-Roger is known to members of M.S.I.A. as the physical manifestation of the Mystical Traveler Consciousness, an all-powerful inner spirit that guides the progress of soul travelers. (This concept, by the way, is quite similar to the Satguru in the Radhasoami tradition and the Mahanta in Twitchell's group.) According to Roger's account, the mantleship of the MTC was passed on to him in or around 1963.[6] During this time, Roger claims to have met Sawan Singh, the late Radhasoami Satsang Beas master who died in 1948. "J.R.," as Hinkins is affectionately called, holds that Sawan Singh was the previous receptor of the

MTC and passed on the "keys" to the Kingdom to him on the inner spiritual planes. In the beginning, however, J.R. did not recognize the luminous being as Sawan Singh. At first, he alleged to be in communication with Rebazar Tarzs, a 500 year old Tibetan monk, who, as it turns out, was a fictional character created by Paul Twitchell to hide his past associations.[7] Accordingly, it was only later when Roger saw a photograph of the Radhasoami guru that he placed the picture of Sawan Singh with the powerful entity he encountered in meditation.[8]

John-Roger's group has grown considerably in the last ten years, and now has centers throughout the United States and in several countries across the globe. M.S.I.A. publishes its own newspaper, The Movement, and the writings of J.R., including such books as The Sound Current, A Consciousness of Wealth, and The Christ Within. Recently there took place the creation of the John-Roger Foundation, a non-profit, tax-exempt organization which supports J.R.'s numerous activities. This Foundation backs the following enterprises:

1. Public Communication: Educational programs; NOW productions; Book division; The Movement Newspaper; and Audio tape division.

2. Educational Institutions: Insight Transformational Seminars; Koh-E-Nor University; PRANA Theological Seminary and College of Philosophy.

3. Health Treatment Baraka Holistic Center for Therapy and Research. 4. Community and Public Service: Insight Service Training; Insight Service Projects; and Individual Service Projects.

5. Spiritual and Philosophical Service M.S.I.A.; Counseling; Publications

At first glance, John-Roger and his Movement appear to be a viable alternative in today's expanding religious market. The official history of M.S.I.A. goes a long way in trying to portray J.R. and his mission as a great boon for humankind and society. At long last, the West has an authentic master of the Sound Current, one who can convey Eastern wisdom in practical, accessible terms–or so the general membership believes. But, according to a growing number of students of J.R. who have recently defected from the ranks, there is a hidden side to the history and design of M.S.I.A. which displays not a genuine spiritual teacher and a true path to God, but a misguided charlatan who will use anything in his power to achieve his aims. It is, no doubt, a controversial issue but, nevertheless, it is

117

one that demands closer scrutiny. The following series of "allegations," which are at the heart of the scandal, will allow us to determine the ultimate legitimacy and authenticity of J.R.'s mastership.

J.R. is a Plagiarist

Since the inception of M.S.I.A., John-Roger has infused his group with a variety of teachings, practices, and New Age techniques from other spiritual traditions. At times this has been a source of embarrassment because his extensive "borrowing" has occasionally turned out to be blatant plagiarism. For instance, compare M.S.I.A.'s cosmology (as found in The Sound Current by John-Roger, dated 1976) with Twitchell's cosmology (as found in The Spiritual Notebook by Paul Twitchell, dated and copyrighted in 1971):

Paul Twitchell's Cosmology (Region and Sound)

1. Physical (Thunder) 2. Astral (Roar of the Sea) 3. Causal (Tinkle of Bells) 4. Mental (Running Water) 5. Soul (Single Note of Flute) 6. Alakh Lok (Heavy Wind) 7. Alaya Lok (Deep Humming) 8. Hukikat Lok (Thousand Violins) 9. Agam Lok (Music of Woodwinds)

John-Roger's Cosmology (Region and Sound)

1. Physical (Thunder) 2. Astral (Roaring Surf) 3. Causal (Tinkle of Bells) 4. Mental (Running Water) 5. Soul (Sound of Flute) Sound of Wind, Humming Sound, Ten Thousand Violins, Sound of Woodwinds

Roger's cosmology is exactly the same as Paul Twitchell's. This is unusual because of Twitchell's own creative implantations which were uniquely his own. Both of the above schemas represent a radical departure from the Radhasoami esoteric version which was the primary source for Twitchell's understanding of the Sound Current and Surat Shabd Yoga practice.[9]

Not only did J.R. copy from Twitchell's publications (consciously or otherwise), but he also appropriated word for word from other metaphysical texts. Perhaps Roger's most graphic example of plagiarism was from Florence Scovel Shinn's book, The Game of Life and How to Play It, published by

DeVorss & Company and copyrighted in 1925. Take a close look at the following comparisons; not a sentence has been changed:

Florence Scovel Shinn (1925)

God is my unfailing supply, and large sums of money come to me quickly, under grace, in perfect ways.

Every plan my father in heaven has not planned, shall be dissolved and dissipated, and the Divine Idea now comes to pass.

Only that which is true of God is true of me, for I and the Father are ONE.

As I am one with God, I am one with my good, for God is both the Giver and the Gift. I cannot separate the Giver from the gift.

Divine love now dissolves and dissipates every wrong condition in my mind, body and affairs. Divine Love is the most powerful chemical in the universe, and dissolves everything which is not of itself!

Divine Love floods my consciousness with health, and every cell in my body is filled with light.

My eyes are God's eyes, I see with the eyes of spirit. I see clearly the open way; there are no obstacles on my pathway. I see clearly the perfect plan.

John Roger Hinkins (1981) [Affirmations]

"God is my unfailing supply, and large sums of money come to me quickly, under grace, in perfect ways. Every plan my father in Heaven has not planned, shall be dissolved and dissipated. The Divine Idea now comes to pass. Only that which is true of God is true of me, for I and the Father am one. As I am one with God, I am one with my good, for God is both the Giver nd the Gift. I cannot separate the Giver from the Gift. Divine love now dissolves and dissipates every wrong condition in my mind, my body and affairs. Divine Love is the most powerful chemical in the universe and dissolves everything which is not of itself. Divine Love floods my consciousness with health and every cell in my body is filled with Light. My eyes are God's eyes. I see with the eyes of Spirit. I see clearly the open way. There are no obstacles on my pathway. I see clearly the perfect plan."

119

John-Roger appears to have a proclivity for taking other teachings, writings, and practices and developing them as his own. Besides the obvious similarities between Roger's Insight Transformational Seminars and Life Spring (as well as Est) one can see his tendency for "borrowing" in his curious use of the word "Sarmad" as a term for God. It seems likely, given J.R.'s track record in matters of religious shoplifting, that he first learned the word "Sugmad" from Paul Twitchell. However, after his exposure to certain Radhasoami Beas texts (particularly the one entitled Sarmad), he transposed Twitchell's term "Sugmad" (which stands for the Highest Lord) into M.S.I.A.'s "Sarmad." In any case, "Sarmad" is actually the name given for a famous Indian-Jewish saint in the Shabd Yoga tradition who died a martyr because of his claim that he was one with God.[10]

Roger, coincidentally, has also taken over the "Holy Five Names" mantra from the Radhasoami Beas and Ruhani Satsangs. In doing so, though, J.R. has mistakenly rearranged the order in two of the names, betraying his ignorance in understanding Indian terminology.[11] This type of indiscriminate borrowing, at least to practitioners from established centers of Surat Shabd Yoga, shows John-Roger to be an unscrupulous spermologos and his group M.S.I.A. to be a potpourri of unoriginal spiritual teachings. The allegation that J.R. is a plagiarist, to some disciples, looks more and more to be a statement of fact.

J.R. Sexually Manipulates His Disciples

Perhaps the most shocking thing to be alleged about John-Roger by a number of M.S.I.A. members is that he sexually manipulates his disciples into having a homosexual affair, claiming that it is for their best spiritual interests. According to several reports, J.R. has apparently been using his spiritual title in order to have sexual relationships with numerous male disciples.

In this regard, Roger joins the growing ranks of gurus who have crossed the ethical borderline between religious guidance and physical intimacy. This infamous assemblage now includes the likes of Swami Muktananda, who according to William Rodarmor's article in *CoEvolution Quarterly* (Winter 1983), was having numerable sexual encounters with his female followers both in America and India before his death in 1982; Neem Karoli Baba, Richard Alpert's teacher, who is recorded to have had "making out" sessions with some of his female American devotees; and Sathya Sai Baba, perhaps India's most famous mystic, who is described by Tal Brooke (one-time disciple) in Lord of the Air (1979) to be a practicing homosexual.[12]

As sexuality is undoubtedly a personal matter and perhaps a skeleton in most individual's closets, it is not my wish to elaborate any further on this private issue which has turned public within the last decade. However, it should be pointed out that spiritual teachers by necessity must be judged by a high moral standard, for they are allowing themselves to be examples of what other humans can and should be. Though, indeed, gurus are human like the rest of us (and deserve our understanding and forgiveness), they represent a higher potential, a supposed enlightened state. Hence, when one does "fall off the pedestal" it should not be ignored or condoned with lame excuses. To do so only allows for more ethical transgressions to occur. Gurus don't hesitate to point out their devotee's weaknesses, nor should disciples be hesitant in criticizing their teacher's faults. Critical exchange is crucial and healthy for any type of relationship– including teacher/students ones.

J.R. is a Charlatan

According to many disenchanted followers, though J.R. claims to be the manifestation of the Mystical Traveler Consciousness he exhibits many of the qualities of a charlatan. Questions have been raised about Roger's lifestyle, business practices, and way of dealing with people.

For instance, it appears that M.S.I.A. (presumably with J.R.'s knowledge) has illegally used the Atman Travel Agency to secure discounts on flights for staff members and other interested parties. The way this is done is to introduce a staff member as a full-time travel agent. But, in most cases, the individual does not work in that capacity, thereby deriving benefit for a service never rendered.[13]

This type of questionable activity extends even to J.R.'s Mandeville Canyon property. When the city of Los Angeles' Department of buildings and Safety sent a letter to John-Roger Hinkins to discontinue the operation of commercial ventures on his residential property, it appears that J.R. (under guidance from his attorney) tried to hide the business dealings going on at Mandeville. This included, among other things, the claim by Roger's lawyer to Senior Building-Mechanical Inspector (J.

Anderson) that "editing" on tapes and books, etc., was a "hobby"–though obviously this was not the case.[14]

J.R.'s personal lifestyle can best be described as luxurious. He has at his disposal hundreds of thousands of dollars for a number of projects. Though he claims to have taken a vow of poverty, Roger lives quite expensively, having the latest in technology and comfort.

Though the preceding sections only partially describe the hidden side of John-Roger, they do bring to focus the important question of whether or not J.R. has any genuine spiritual authority or if his group M.S.I.A. is at all a legitimate and authentic enterprise.

What About Credentials? The Traditional Analysis

There are two major ways that one can judge the legitimacy of a spiritual movement: from inside the tradition and outside of it. Our critical analysis, therefore, will be on these two fronts, first utilizing the principles of Sant Mat, Radhasoami, and Shabd Yoga for the practical critique; and secondly, applying the evaluations of transpersonal psychology (via Wilber and Welwood) for the external appraisement.

Since John-Roger readily admits that Sawan Singh, the late Radhasoami Beas guru, was the previous receptor of the Mystical Traveler Consciousness, it is only natural for our purposes to see if J.R. himself lives up to the guidelines of a true master, as posited by Sawan Singh and his predecessors.[15] (It should be noted that Sawan Singh [1858-1948] was a highly esteemed master of Shabd Yoga "union of the soul with the Divine Sound" in North India and had a very large following. His guru was Jaimal Singh, the spiritual successor of Shiv Dayal Singh, who founded the Radhasoami path in the mid 19th century in Agra, India.) Below are the results of the comparison:

[Sawan Singh]

1. True masters never charge money for their services in any form (this, of course, includes membership or initiation). Nor do they live off the offerings of their disciples. True masters are self-supporting.

2. True masters must be initiated themselves while in the body by a genuine guru. Successorship, naturally, necessitates

an acknowledgement on behalf of the departing master of his heir.

3. True masters are strict vegetarians and insist that their disciples do the same.

4. True masters do not drink alcohol nor take mind-altering drugs.

5. True masters do not claim psychic powers or perform public miracles.

6. True masters only have sexual relations with their spouse.

[John Roger]

1. M.S.I.A., under the direction of J.R., charges a yearly rate for membership. (Initiation generally can only be secured if you are a member first.) John-Roger, though he claims to have taken a vow of poverty, has used thousands of dollars of his group's money for his own uses.

2. John-Roger disavows having taken initiation from any Shabd Yoga master while living in the physical body (including Sawan Singh, who had been deceased for fifteen years when J.R. claims to have met him).

3. John-Roger is a meat-eater. M.S.I.A. students do not take a vow of vegetarianism.

4. John-Roger is reported to consume alcoholic beverages and take a variety of legal prescription drugs.

5. John-Roger, on occasion, claims psychic ability.

6. John-Roger, according to a number of disciples, has sexually manipulated several males into affairs.

As is made obvious from the above analysis, John-Roger would not be regarded as a genuine master by Sawan Singh and the Sant Mat tradition. Rather, he has all the earmarks of a guru not to follow. This is further supported by the illuminating fact that Roger's spiritual and meditational advice is almost always opposite that given by Sawan Singh and other saints in India:

[Sawan Singh]

A) A disciple of a perfect master once initiated can never be uninitiated or disconnected from the Sound Current or his guru. He is, in the course of time, assured of his destination, God-realization.

B) Test the form that may appear in meditation by repeating the Holy Names given to them at the time of their initiation.

[John Roger]

A)"Your reconnections to the Sound Current did not hold and this is to notify you that you are no longer initiates of the Mystical Traveler and of the Sound Current."–letter from the Movement Board,[16] under the direction of J.R.

B) Advises his disciples not to repeat their Holy Tones when they encounter inner beings during their meditations.

In light of Sant Mat principles and history, John-Roger's story about receiving the mantleship of the Mystical Traveler Consciousness and contacting Sawan Singh on the inner planes, etc., cannot be taken seriously, as it would contradict the very teachings of Sawan Singh and Shabd Yoga. Hence, in this context, J.R. has no proof or rightful demand for his spiritual authority. Likewise, neither does M.S.I.A. (as a religious organization under the direction of Roger) have any substantial claim for being a true source or lineage for Sound Current practices and doctrines.[17]

The Humanistic and Transpersonal Critique

Due to the pioneering work of Ken Wilber and John Welwood,[18] it is now possible to critically analyze new religious movements and their leaders from a humanistic/transpersonal perspective.

If we apply Wilber's scale of legitimacy and authenticity to John-Roger, for example, we find that J.R. has a very weak case for his mastership, since he lacks both a documented historical lineage and outside confirmation from other well-established Sound Current teachers. Concurrently, M.S.I.A., since it springs solely out of J.R.'s own creative enterprising, scores a low rating in legitimacy also.[19]

In terms of authenticity (the actual transformative powers of the group), there can be no question that M.S.I.A. does ultimately aim for higher realms of consciousness and that some sincere individuals may be achieving those exalted states. However, these experiences have nothing to do, per se, with John-Roger or M.S.I.A. Rather, as I have arguedelsewhere,[20] it is the person's own inherent capability for transcendent insights that enables one to have inner visions and out-of-body experiences. This is most acutely exemplified in the reports of near-death patients who describe beautiful encounters with a being of light. The NDE experience, as Moody, Ring, and Sabom have indicated in their research, is a transcultural phenomenon, available to any person no matter what religion or country they may belong to.[21]

Thus, following this line of reasoning, it would be erroneous for M.S.I.A. initiates who have mystical encounters to assume that John-Roger is necessarily the cause for it. Instead, it is one's own belief, faith, concentration, and potential for further structural adaptation which has acted as the catalyst for the elevation.[22] This does not mean, though, that true masters do not administer spiritual benefit to their disciples, but only that the individual must first allow for further insight and advancement. Enlightenment, as Wilber so aptly points out, cannot be forced upon people–only slavery can.

Another important appraisement of spiritual masters and groups comes from John Welwood's classic article, "On Spiritual Authority: Genuine and Counterfeit," which appeared in the *Journal of Humanistic Psychology* (Summer 1983). Welwood draws an important distinction between genuine and counterfeit gurus by illustrating the differences between Egocentricity and Being. Diagrams Welwood [23]:

[Egocentricity]

Concern with maintaining appearances; concern with maintaining and validating a self-image; contraction around "I-ness"; sense of insecurity and inadequacy;

[Being]

Concern with discovering truth; interest in and appreciation of the world, independently of how it affirms or negates any self-image; expansion outward toward life and the phenomenal world; basic sense of wholeness, well-being, aliveness, and intelligence

If we accept the picture of John-Roger that has been drawn by a number of ex-followers (and outlined throughout this article) and place it through Welwood's grid, it becomes obvious that J.R. has more traits of Egocentricity than of Being. This will become even clearer when we review Roger's reactions to criticism.

The Red Monk Disease

The most telling sign of whether a master is genuine or fraudulent, authentic or counterfeit, filled with Ego or Being, is to see how he reacts to personal criticism. It is easy to "look" majestic and benevolent when everyone around is adoring you. But, the real test is to find out how the guru responds in a negative situation. Only then can a disciple witness the real merits of his teacher.

How does John-Roger stand up on the face of adverse publicity? Not very well it seems. For instance, when word got out that several disciples were talking about his personal/hidden life, J.R. immediately tried to squelch it by having his lawyers send letters pointing out the possible legal ramifications if they persisted. Not satisfied with just a conventional defense, Roger also declared to his membership that certain wayward students were now embodying the "Red Monk," a negative delusion, etc. Declares a letter from the Movement Board to one of these "straying" followers:

"We will also once again be notifying those people that ask that you are once again embodying the Negative Power in the form of the Red Monk and the consequences that goes with this power. Please understand that this action is not against you but for those whom you would once again contaminate with this energy field. Most of the people in the Movement who have contacted us have noticed the peculiar actions around you that reminded them of the occurrences when your egos led you into patterns of deceit and half truths in the past."

What does this "Red Monk" do? According to the Movement Board it contaminates anything which comes into its field of energy. Who are the most likely candidates for the dreaded disorder? Students who criticize John-Roger or M.S.I.A. To show to what extent John-Roger will go in defending his actions, I have included some excerpts from letters that have been written on his behalf or M.S.I.A.'s to dissident students.

It has come to my attention that you and other individuals have been slandering and invading the privacy of several of my clients including John-Roger, the Church of the Movement of Spiritual Awareness...and others involved therewith...As attorney for these individuals and foundations, I have been instructed to request that you immediately cease and desist from said activities.

I direct your attention to California Civil Code Section 43 et seq. and related cases involving the possible penalties for your actions... (Letter from attorney Marc Darrow on behalf of John-Roger)

This is to inform you that I am no longer in support of you being a minister in the Movement of Spiritual Inner Awareness and so I am requesting that you hand in your Ministerial ordination and pocket size credentials as soon as possible. Since you have effectively placed yourself under the power of the Kal power and its field of negativity known as the Red Monk I can also no longer support you as an initiate and ask that you request to have this relationship terminated... (Letter from John-Roger to a former minister and student of M.S.I.A.)

What emerges from these letters is not a compassionate and forgiving spiritual teacher, but a resentful, obviously insecure individual who possesses the failings of a common man. John-Roger, and not his questioning disciples, appears to be suffering from a bad case of over-exposure to the fearful Red Monk disease. The only cure available for J.R., it seems, is to concede to the fact that he is more a charlatan than a saint.

POSTSCRIPT (1993)

This article was originally written in 1983 after I was approached by several highly placed members of M.S.I.A. who felt betrayed by John-Roger Hinkins. Since I was somewhat friendly with J.R. (we had met on several occasions at his home about my research on Paul Twitchell, shabd yoga, and Radhasoami), I called him on the telephone to get his response to the three main allegations made against him (plagiarism, sexual manipulation, and charlatanism). J.R. did not take kindly to my questions and did not want me to do any further research on him. Indeed, after that phone conversation in the Fall of 1983 I was subjected to a series of threats, including several made against my life and the lives of my friends/informants.

The situation reached a peak the following year on October 5, 1984, when my home was ransacked and a number of my research files were purloined. Documentary evidence (outlined in a special issue of UCSM entitled "The Criminal Activities of John-Roger Hinkins") implicates John-Roger with the Del Mar robbery, as well as engineering a smear campaign replete with death threats against his critics. Subsequently major news organizations began to investigate J.R. A number of provocative articles were published which exposed John-Roger in a negative light, including an extensive two part critique in *The Los Angeles Times*.

It should be noted, however, that when The J.R. Controversy first appeared I had to go to press without using the names of my informants, each of who declined to go public because they feared for their safety. Thus, even though my critique was the first of its kind ever done on J.R. and the Movement, I was more or less a sitting duck for his retaliatory efforts. J.R. waged a systematic campaign against me by setting up a phony front organization entitled the "Coalition for Civil and Spiritual Rights." In order to mail out his threatening letters, J.R. rented a mail box in West Los Angeles under three pseudonyms: Peter Davidson, Ph.D., Michael Hunt, and Kip Ferguson. J.R. made one devastating mistake, though, in creating his front: he personally paid and signed for the mail box, betraying in one stroke of the pen his claim that he was not aware of C.C.S.R.

After discovering J.R.'s plot (and after receiving some of the stolen materials back which contained John-Roger's handwriting in the margins), I wrote another article which detailed his criminal activities. I also went on a couple of television programs, including the nationally syndicated Now It Can Be Told, and mentioned on air how J.R. was involved in a number of illegal dealings. Since all of my allegations were based upon extensive documentation, J.R. has never taken any legal action. The ironic twist in all of this, however, is that J.R. is now more popular than ever. This is primarily due to his co-authoring a number of bestselling books, with such catchy titles as Life 101 and Wealth 101. Despite a flurry of negative publicity around the world (the U.K. press has been especially hard on John-Roger and his Movement), J.R. has shown a remarkable resilience to rebound from adversity.

NOTES

1. See "Transcendental Sociology."
2. Personal interview with John-Roger Hinkins at his home in Mandeville Canyon (1978). Also refer to the May 12, 1973 issue of the *Movement Newspaper* which elaborates on J.R.'s association with Paul Twitchell.
3. Writes an ex-member of M.S.I.A., in a personal letter to the author (dated November 15, 1983): "You may be interested to know that years

ago Roger Hinkins studied with a small group in Glendale, CA that still exists called the Fellowship of Universal Guidance. Some of us went there recently to hear one of their classes which consists of information about the 3 selves and the Christ. I believe Roger Hinkins very cleverly devised a saleable package by combining the material from [Paul Twitchell and his movement] with the material from this group. . . ."

4. An example of this is Roger's acceptance of Twitchell's unusual claim that the sound of the "flute" is heard on the soul plane and that the "tinkling of bells" is audible in the casual region. No shabd yoga tradition in India connected to Radhasoami has ever stated such a thing; rather, they make reference to the sound of a "vina" (or bagpipe) in Sach Khand and the "conch" (or drum) in Trikuti, the casual plane.

5. Paul Twitchell's group is also aware of this similarity and at one time threatened lawsuits against J.R. for his actions. Memos against M.S.I.A. have been sent out by Twitchell and his attorneys.

6. Personal interview with John-Roger Hinkins at his home in Mandeville Canyon (1978-1979). The latter interview has since been transcribed by John-Roger and copied.

7. See my book, *The Making of a Spiritual Movement* (Del Mar: Del Mar Press, 1994).

8. Personal interview with John-Roger Hinkins, op. cit.

9. This connection between Radhasoami and American Sound Current teachings is outlined in my paper "The New Panths: Shabdism in North America," which was first presented to the American Academy of Religion at Stanford University in 1982. It has subsequently been incorporated in my book *The Making of a Spiritual Movement* (op. cit.). Also see "Bhrigu Samhita."

10. Refer to Isaac A. Ezekiel's *Sarmad: The Jewish Saint of India* (Beas: Radha Soami Foundation).

11. Personal interview with John-Roger Hinkins (op. cit.) where he revealed the "Holy Five Names" to me off tape. Also this information was confirmed by several ex-members of M.S.I.A.

12. In early 1983 at a dinner date in San Diego, California, I had the opportunity to speak with author Tal Brooke about Sathya Sai Baba's alleged homosexual advances. Brooke informed me that Sathya Sai Baba had made a "pass" at him, overtly trying to handle his genitals. Undoubtedly this is a controversial issue, but one which is coming more into the limelight each day. Below is a list of gurus who are reported to have had sexual affairs with their disciples in some way: 1) John-Roger Hinkins; 2) Sathya Sai Baba; 3) Thakar Singh; 4) Neem Karoli Baba; 5) Zen abbot Dick Baker; 6) Swami Muktananda; 7) Swami Rama; and Frederick Lenz (Rama).

13. Interviews with ex-members of M.S.I.A. Also refer to the television program, "Now It Can Be Told" (Fall 1991), which records on tape the various allegations made against J.R.

14. Ibid.

15. Refer to Julian P. Johnson's *The Path of the Masters* (Beas: Radha Soami Foundation, 1939)–excerpts of which are included in the last note–and Sawan Singh's Spiritual Gems (Beas: Radha Soami Foundation, 1965).

16. Interviews with former students of J.R.

17. For more on the history of shabd yoga and the lineages of Sant Mat and Radhasoami masters please refer to Mark Juergensmeyer's *Radhasoami Reality* (Princeton: Princeton University Press, 1991) and this author's *The Radhasoami Tradition* (New York & London: Garland Publishing, 1992).

18. See Ken Wilber's *A Sociable God* (New York: McGraw-Hill, 1983) and Eye to Eye (New York: Doubleday / Anchor Press, 1983).

19. Ken Wilber, op. cit.

20. Please refer to *The Unknowing Sage: The Life and Work of Baba Faqir Chand* (Walnut: Mount San Antonio College Press, 1993).

21. Ibid.

22. Ibid.

23. John Welwood, "On Spiritual Authority: Genuine and Counterfeit," *Journal of Humanistic Psychology* (Summer 1983, page 50).

James Lewis on John-Roger's Past [from Seeking the Light]

He held down a number of jobs, including a short stint in the coal mines. While in college, he worked as a night orderly in the psychiatric ward of a Salt Lake City hospital. Later he held a part-time job as a PBX telephone operator and dispatcher with the Salt Lake City Police Department. After completing a degree in psychology at the University of Utah in 1958, he moved to southern California and eventually took a job teaching English at Rosemead High School.

The turning point of his life occurred in 1963, during what we might today call a near-death experience. While undergoing surgery for a kidney stone, he fell into a nine-day coma. Upon awakening, he found himself aware of a new spiritual personality 'John' who had superseded merged with his old personality. After the operation, Hinkins began to refer to himself as 'John-Roger,' in recognition of his transformed self.

Around this time John-Roger was a seeker exploring a variety of different spiritual teachings, including Eckankar, a Sant Mat-inspired group. Parallels between Eckankar and the Movement of Spiritual Inner Awareness have prompted critics to accuse him of plagiarizing Eckankar. During an interview with J-R, I asked him about his relationship with Paul Twitchell, the founder of Eckankar. His response was:

I've been asked, 'Were you a student of Eckankar?' Yeah, if you can consider I was a student of the Reader's Digest and National Geographic and the Rosecrucians and some other churches all at the same time. I went to some of the churches to see what they did–[I was what they refer to as] a metaphysical tramp. I call those my 'meta-fizzle' days because none of those ever worked out.

HI FUBBI, THIS IS GAKKO
Excerpt from The San Diego Reader's Cover story on Eckankar
(1995)

Lane decided against pursuing a lawsuit against Hinkins, but he did go public with his story. In Understanding Cults Lane published "The Criminal Activities of John-Roger Hinkins," a laborious account of Hinkins' alleged break-in and smear campaign. He also gave full accounts to the San Diego Sheriff's Department and to numerous news agencies. "On the Marie Vega Show in Los Angeles, I said, 'John-Roger Hinkins robbed my house.' He threatened to sue the TV station for a million dollars if they ever ran the program again. But they kept running it, and he never sued them." In August 1988, The Los Angeles Times published an extensive two-part critique of John-Roger's activities, based on Lane's research. Lane also appeared on Geraldo Rivera's Now It Can Be Told. "Geraldo was in New York and I was on satellite hook-up at Universal Studios in San Fernando Valley. 'The Cadillac of Cults. Are your tax dollars being spent by this group?'

So they interviewed me, and I had this rainbow tie on, and Geraldo and I were going at each other. I said, 'Yeah, Geraldo, this guy robbed my house, he did this he did this he did that'–all on national TV. I just went off on him. At this stage Peter McWilliams, the guy who later wrote *Life 102*, was still pro-John-Roger, so he was putting his hands on the camera, that kind of scene, when they tried to interview John-Roger. So you get this juxtaposition, Lane really going off on John-Roger and McWilliams trying to protect J.R.'s reputation."

After such an exhausting chronicle, I feebly inquire, "Are you still doing research on John-Roger?"

Lane takes a deep breath. "No."

About the Authors

Andrea Diem-Lane is a Professor of Philosophy at Mt. San Antonio College. She received her Ph.D. and M.A. in Religious Studies from the University of California, Santa Barbara, where she did her doctoral studies under Professor Ninian Smart. Professor Diem received a B.A. in Psychology with an emphasis on Brain Research from the University of California, San Diego, where she did pioneering visual cortex research under the tutelage of Dr. V.S. Ramachandran. Dr. Diem is the author of several books including an interactive textbook on religion entitled *How Scholars Study the Sacred* and an interactive book on the famous Einstein-Bohr debate over the implications of quantum theory entitled *Spooky Physics*. Her most recent book is *Darwin's DNA: An Introduction to Evolutionary Philosophy*.

David Christopher Lane is a Professor of Philosophy at Mt. San Antonio College and an Adjunct Lecturer in Science and Religion at California State University, Long Beach. He received his Ph.D. in the Sociology of Knowledge from the University of California, San Diego, where he was also a recipient of a Regents Fellowship. He has taught previously at Warren College at UCSD, the University of London, and the California School of Professional Psychology. He has given invited lectures at various universities, including the London School of Economics. He is the author of a number of published books such as The *Making of a Spiritual Movement: The Untold Story of Paul Twitchell and Eckankar*; The *Radhasoami Tradition: A Critical History of Guru Succession*; *Exposing Cults: When the Skeptical Mind Confronts the Mystical*; and *The Unknowing Sage: The Life and Work of Baba Faqir Chand*, among others.